USING POWER WELL

USING POWER WELL

BOB WILLIAMS and the MAKING of BRITISH COLUMBIA

BOB WILLIAMS

with BENJAMIN ISITT and THOMAS BEVAN

NIGHTWOOD EDITIONS

Nightwood Editions
P.O. Box 1779
Gibsons, BC VON 1V0
Canada
www.nightwoodeditions.com

COVER DESIGN: Topshelf Creative
TYPOGRAPHY: Carleton Wilson

Nightwood Editions acknowledges the support of the Canada Council for the Arts, the Government of Canada, and the Province of British Columbia through the BC Arts Council.

This book has been produced on 100% post-consumer recycled, ancient-forest-free paper, processed chlorine-free and printed with vegetable-based dyes.

Printed and bound in Canada.

LIBRARY AND ARCHIVES CANADA CATALOGUING IN PUBLICATION

Title: Using power well : Bob Williams and the making of British Columbia / Bob Williams, with Benjamin Isitt and Thomas Bevan.
Other titles: Bob Williams and the making of British Columbia
Names: Williams, Bob, 1933- author. | Isitt, Benjamin, 1978- author. | Bevan, Thomas (Urban planner), author.
Identifiers: Canadiana (print) 20220154570 | Canadiana (ebook) 20220154600 | ISBN 9780889714243 (softcover) | ISBN 9780889714250 (EPUB)
Subjects: LCSH: Williams, Bob, 1933- | LCSH: Politicians—British Columbia—Biography. | LCSH: British Columbia—Politics and government—20th century. | LCGFT: Autobiographies.
Classification: LCC FC3827.1.W55 A3 2022 | DDC 971.1/04092—dc23

For Lea, and all the women who made the difference

CONTENTS

PREFACE

I know I must do this. There are so few of us left with relatively clear memories, who still have our heads in half-decent shape. I feel I have a responsibility to the greats that came before me. As a young historian at ICBC said to me years ago, "You've got to write, Bob, or they'll steal it from you." Amen, sister! It's not just the projects. It's the nuances, the background, the passion, the chaos, the growth, the camaraderie and a very unique group of people who for a while, changed our world here in British Columbia.

So several years ago, I took a month off my various projects in Vancouver and headed down to the Florida Keys and Arizona. Freed of daily chores and distractions, I rested enough to free my mind and memory, and brought along an empty journal to be filled. Amid tropical birds, flowers and the warm breeze off the sea and desert, I filled the journal with handwritten musings and memories from a life in planning and politics. During this month-long writing retreat, I was up before dawn most days, awaking to unlock and unpack these boxcars of memory. It was like being back in our house on Wall Street in East Vancouver, above the CPR tracks with the shunting of freight. I think it is REM sleep that frees both the subconscious and memory. They're surely linked. Each morning, the memories would return, first slowly, then in a flood. Tapping the subconscious led to memory, then to writing it down. And then using another part of the brain to provide a kind of analysis.

I suspect that some readers will object to my observations, analyses and opinions. My choice of words in some chapters is admittedly hard-hitting, providing cutting criticism of former colleagues both living and dead. I have reflected on these sections at length, contemplating the use of more restrained language. Some sections have been revised to avoid seeming harsh and unfair. In other sections I have chosen to retain the sharpness of my criticism, to offer current and future generations an unvarnished, undiluted perspective on the process of struggle and change within our public institutions, as I experienced and saw it. If anyone believes they have been unfairly represented in these memoirs, my apologies. I take full responsibility for any omissions and any errors of fact or analysis.

One morning in Arizona, during a brief break from writing these memoirs, I slipped out onto the patio. Desert dawn is so special, and a desert bird was singing away out there in a neighbour's orange tree. He continued greeting the dawn for another five minutes, sharing his voice with me, undisturbed, maybe pleased, by my presence. What a pleasure!

Bob Williams

INTRODUCTION

It has been our privilege to assist in a small way in helping Bob Williams tell his important story. Thomas first met Bob in 2011, when he was completing his master of planning degree in the same program as Bob at the University of British Columbia, but sixty years later. Bob was a guest speaker telling stories of his awe-inspiring career as a city builder to a group of starry-eyed students. Subsequently, Bob and Thomas worked together on several projects over the next decade.

Ben first met Bob at a municipal conference in 2015. An informal conversation over forest policy led Ben to help Bob organize his personal papers for donation and preservation at the University of British Columbia's special collections. After the transport of thirty boxes of documents across the Salish Sea and back, the discussion evolved over the course of several interviews and culminated in Ben editing Bob's handwritten memoirs for publication. This book is the product of that collaboration.

Several people played integral roles in the creation of this book, including research assistants who transcribed and organized interviews and records—Vincent Gornall, Thomas Woodsworth, Elysia Glover and Stephen Russo—and the competent team at Nightwood Editions, particularly Silas White and Emma Skagen. Rob Douglas provided the original introduction for Bob and Ben, sparking the opportunity for this collaboration. Mary Rawson, Am Johal, Denis O'Gorman and Charles Barber all provided invaluable input. The Jim Green Foundation generously provided resources for this work, helping advance ideas of social and economic democracy and the principles of economist Henry George. We would like to express our appreciation to everyone who has played a role in the preparation of this book.

As Bob writes in the pages that follow, he learned that "the job of the good politician was to use power well." We will leave it to the judgment of others to determine whether or not Bob Williams used power well—in his most high-profile position as British Columbia's minister of lands, forests and water resources in the 1970s, in previous positions as the municipality of Delta's first town planner and as a Vancouver city alderman, and more recently in leadership positions in the provincial Crown Corporations secretariat, the Insurance Corporation of British Columbia and the Vancouver City Savings Credit Union (Vancity). To be sure, Bob is a controversial figure on the province's political landscape. His inclination to be a "straight shooter," as he describes it, who "truly tells it as it is" with "no bullshit," has probably made him more enemies than friends.

But love him or hate him, Bob Williams has left his mark on British Columbia. He was born in 1933 and raised by working-class parents in Burnaby and Vancouver. Educated as an economist and urban planner at the University of British Columbia in the 1950s, Bob would go on to work as the municipality of Delta's first town planner—attracting controversy for refusing to approve sprawling subdivisions on agricultural land. He was elected to serve as a Vancouver city alderman (1964–1966), working across partisan lines to challenge the political power of the business community and advance an alternate vision for the city—including opposing so-called urban renewal, and a freeway that was proposed to run through the East Side and downtown.

Municipal office served as a springboard to provincial politics, with Bob winning election as one of two members of the legislative assembly (MLAs) from the then multiple-member riding of Vancouver East in 1966. He ran unsuccessfully for the provincial New Democratic Party leadership in 1969, and for much of his time in provincial politics he served as chair of the party's legislative caucus. In 1972, after Dave Barrett led the NDP to power for the first time in the province's history, Bob was appointed the minister of lands, forests and water resources, as well as minister of recreation and conservation.

Bob exercised substantial influence over government policy in this role; he acted as the closest confidant to the premier during that government's brief three-year tenure, when nearly four hundred pieces of legislation were enacted—a more aggressive legislative record than the preceding Social Credit government had undertaken during its two decades in power. Deploying his expertise in economics and planning, and a Georgist approach to land and resource rents, Bob led the Environment and Land Use Committee of cabinet and its secretariat (ELUC), enlisting a team of path-breaking professional colleagues to work in this policy arm of the new government. Bob describes his work during the thirty-eight-month tenure of the Barrett government as the most exhausting and exhilarating period of his life.

Following the NDP's defeat in 1975, Bob stepped aside as Vancouver East MLA to provide a path for Barrett, who had narrowly lost his Coquitlam seat, to return to the legislature. Bob worked as a researcher for the NDP caucus, then focused for a time on business and real estate, including operating the Barnet Motor Inn in Port Moody, Sisto's Pub in Mission and Vancouver's iconic Railway Club nightclub, an innovative cultural space where stars including k.d. lang enjoyed their first exposure in Vancouver. Bob returned as Vancouver East MLA in a 1984 by-election, when Barrett retired from provincial politics. Bob continued to advocate for transformation in the management of natural resources on the opposition benches until 1991.

That year, when the NDP returned to power, Bob led the transition team for Mike Harcourt and was appointed deputy minister of the Crown Corporations secretariat, helping steer provincial resource policy once again. He served as chair of the board of the Insurance Corporation of British Columbia (ICBC) from 1998 to 2001, spearheading Surrey's Central City project. And in his most sustained political project ever, Bob led the transformation of the Vancity credit union as a director, chair and advisor from 1983 to 2016. In this role, Bob was influential in Vancity's rise to Canada's largest financial co-operative, and he stewarded an annual educational program on co-operative economics with the University of Bologna in Italy's Emilia-Romagna region.

The historical record and the province's public policy environment are dotted with the contributions of Bob Williams and those around him—including the Agricultural Land Reserve, the Insurance Corporation of British Columbia, the Islands Trust, the Resort Municipality of Whistler, the British Columbia Assessment Authority, BC Housing, Robson Square, the SeaBus and West Coast Express public transit systems, the Columbia Basin Trust, Simon Fraser University's Surrey campus, and, more recently, the development of 312 Main, Vancouver's centre for social and economic innovation.

Some of Bob's ideas for advancing the public interest in British Columbia never came to fruition. For example, around 1973 he approached Premier Dave Barrett, proposing that the Government of British Columbia purchase Rolls-Royce, the British engine and luxury car manufacturer. As Bob tells it, the company was woefully undervalued in the international financial market, and he insists to this day that purchasing the company would have been a smart investment for provincial taxpayers, with far-reaching strategic benefits to advance the industrial and manufacturing sectors of the provincial economy. But in one of the few instances where Barrett appears to have said no to his lieutenant and long-time friend, the premier told Bob that they were not going to buy Rolls-Royce on behalf of the people of BC. This story demonstrates Bob's unconventional approach to policy and governance, which seems to have always operated outside the institutional and ideological straitjackets that are so common in the wardrobes of public figures—both at the time that Bob served as minister and in the more recent neoliberal cultural context of twenty-first-century British Columbia politics.

Bob Williams is something of an enigma and a contradiction from the standpoint of ideology and working-class politics, defying conventional interpretations from liberalism to Marxism and beyond. His public policy outputs as minister of lands, forests and water resources display an inherent radicalism and socialist worldview—having the effect of shifting power and resources away from private property interests and toward collective interests. But Bob also exemplifies success in the commercial fields of business, real estate and banking at different points in his life, including as the long-standing owner of the Railway Club, a Vancouver cultural icon.

"I should make it clear that I am in favour of private tenure," Bob said in a speech at a 1993 conference of the Union of Russian Mayors as the country debated its post-Soviet future. "I am convinced that private tenure is necessary if you are to achieve your full potential. Defining tenure, however, and defining rents is absolutely critical if you want to avoid the worst extremes ... and achieve a reasonable level of fairness in the distribution of wealth in your society." Bob urged the Russians to retain public ownership of the central business districts of their cities, to collect annual rents exceeding the total expenditures of local governments, removing the need for tax revenues. This robust application of resource rents reflected the intellectual impact of the radical American economist Henry George, whose philosophy Bob first encountered as a young economics student at UBC; George's influence would go on to shape Bob's later work as a planner and politician.

The radical socialist collectivist impulse in Bob's approach to public policy can also be traced to his lineage. His personal story connects with key moments in the development of the labour and left-wing traditions in British Columbia. Bob's great-grandfather James Pritchard immigrated from northern England to work as a coal miner in robber baron James Dunsmuir's Nanaimo mines at the dawn of the twentieth century. He helped organize the workers in those mines and spearhead the formation of the Socialist Party of Canada, which held the balance of power in the provincial legislature before the First World War.

Bob's grandfather William A. Pritchard (James's son) would go on to lead the breakaway One Big Union. He was incarcerated for more than a year in a federal prison farm in Manitoba after being convicted of seditious conspiracy in connection with the Winnipeg General Strike of 1919. In the 1930s, Pritchard was elected to serve as reeve (mayor) of Burnaby. When he refused to cut off relief payments to unemployed residents, pushing the municipality into a fiscal deficit, the provincial government fired Pritchard and his council, appointing a trustee to run the municipality until midway through the Second World War. So,

Bob came by his radical beliefs and rejection of established institutions honestly.

Bob's personal life is complex. As he recounts in these memoirs, he was estranged from his birth father for a number of years, grappling with his identity as a teenager when he learned about the circumstances surrounding his birth. Bob was married at the age of thirty-seven to party activist Lea Forsyth (who had two children from a previous marriage, Janet and Stephen), and together they had a daughter, Suzanne. After three decades of marriage, Bob came out as gay, but he never discussed his sexual orientation in public. His decision to step down as Vancouver East MLA prior to the 1991 election was influenced by a thinly veiled threat from the ruling Social Credit party machine to expose him as a closeted homosexual.

As editors, we have endeavoured to retain Bob's voice and focus, aiming for a light touch that preserves Bob's own words, opinions, perspectives and experiences. In addition, we note that this book is not supplemented with original archival research into the events, personalities, organizations and initiatives that Bob discusses. A rigorous scholarly examination of Bob Williams's contribution to the making of modern British Columbia is therefore the topic for another work—perhaps a graduate thesis and subsequent monograph.

We chose to assist in telling Bob's story because we believe that readers will find his own perspective valuable in understanding the political path he chose to pursue, the decisions that he made and the public policy outcomes that arose from his strong will and his evident intellectual capacity. We invite you to join him in envisioning the kind of province he believes is possible and strategies for getting there—bypassing bureaucracies and using power well.

Benjamin Isitt and Thomas Bevan

1. WORKING-CLASS ROOTS

I've felt the need for some time to describe my early days in the glorious Vancouver region. My generation was the exact opposite of the baby boomers because the 1930s were not exactly boom times and, indeed, few people were born then. We were poor, and even as kids we knew it—but it didn't matter very much. Vancouver was a special place to grow up, and the poverty actually made everything more exciting in what would now be seen as a hopelessly difficult era.

Before I went to school, we lived near the city dump in Still Creek (now the Italian Cultural Centre) where I loved to join our Ukrainian neighbour in sorting garbage to make a few pennies. "Find the right bottles, kid. They're worth something," he would say to me. I learned fast, and I even made some money. My dad complained a little when I came home smelling of both the dump and the garlic-laden lunch that the family had spread out for me. I may have even picked up some soot from trains shunting through the Great Northern Railway cut, where I would end the workday sprawled out on the cliff above, daydreaming and reflecting on the good day's work with my buddy.

I was the oldest kid, so it was my job to cut the kindling, light the fire in the wood stove and get the porridge cooking. I liked doing those chores, even on the coldest winter days. What I didn't like was having to babysit my younger brother and sister whenever my folks went out. I frequently avoided my babysitting job by being rescued by Nana, my mother's mother, who wanted me with her when she headed out across the inlet to Dollarton to camp alone as a widow. Camp was a happy escape for both of us.

Nana lived at 715 Gilmore Avenue South in North Burnaby. We would take off from there, up the plank sidewalk to Hastings Street where we would catch the Hastings Extension, a streetcar that was an extension from the Boundary Road Terminus of the Number 14 streetcar. The extension went to the top of Capitol Hill. The motorman liked to crank it up to top speed and it lurched and swayed most of the way—rarely having to stop—most people walking all the way from Boundary Road. At Capitol Hill School, we'd hike across the grounds heading for the forested northern escarpment, carrying our supplies in buckets and baskets. Folks living at the bottom of the hill used the trails daily and upgraded them regularly by adding new steps or cutting through windfalls. Lots of little streams on the steep slope provided water for the squatters living in the shacks below.

Our destination was Oscar's shack, along the tracks a way from where the trail ended. Oscar was a Scandinavian boatbuilder who lived in one of the hundreds of shacks built on piling on the north side of the CPR mainline. The area along the North Burnaby shore was called Crabtown. Near to Oscar's home was his own little shipyard, where he produced beautiful little clinker-built rowboats. Nana had been able to buy one of his boats and berth it tethered to the piling near his shack.

Oscar was only one of the many who would generally be seen as down and out, but for me they were fascinating characters who had created a wonderful life for themselves. Some of the shacks were tarted up with bright enamel trim and had fun names above their entries like "Dew Drop Inn" and "The Last Resort." Poverty in Crabtown didn't look too bad: no rent, no taxes, seemingly no government. But there was clearly a sense of community—everyone helped one another with supplies, with water, with working on the trails. In one spot in Crabtown, the residents cleared a small community beach and constructed a barnacled rock pile from the former rubble. The pile of rubble became big enough that the locals named it Coney Island. Coney Island became big enough to build a ramshackle long building that hung out over tidewater at each end. And on most Saturday nights, Crabtown had a dance in their very own community hall. But Crabtown was not our final destination; Nana and I were headed for Dollarton, over on the

North Shore near Roche Point. After very few lessons, I was the one who rowed Nana across to her camp.

All this would have started around 1940, eight decades ago. I was anxious to please Nana. After all, to spend most of your summer holidays at camp, living it up in what was one of the best cottages in a long string of shacks, seemed to me the ultimate privilege for a ten-year-old. "Camp" had started out like most of the other shacks along the shoreline. You got driftwood from the inlet and built yourself a shack. There were logs galore floating in the inlet; they provided the piling for the shack. Stones cleared from the beach were piled to create a barrier to protect the piling and the cottage at high tide and avoid damage from other driftwood. But our place was expanded over the years from one room to two and then three. More than that, there was a veranda on both sides of the house. One deck was extra large in order to prevent other squatters from coming too close. The Hooper family—friends of my parents—had come out for a picnic one Sunday, and Nana was miffed when they decided to build to the west of us. It was then and there that the veranda got enlarged.

Alex and Nancy Chat to the east of us had built their cottage at the same time as my grandfather Arthur de Chasteauneuf. Together the two families cleared the beach, lit fires around the biggest rocks, then split the rocks when the cold waters swirled in at high tide. Next door to the Chats was the Cooper family, who only showed up at the peak of summer. Nana and the Chats were regulars. Whenever there was any free time, they were there. Alex Chat was a tall, well-built Englishman. His wife, Nancy, was a jolly buxom woman who loved life with her family—Alex, Ken and Peter. Peter was about my age but we never had a lot in common. Most of my time was spent with Nana.

With Nana I could be useful collecting firewood and bark along the beach. I could cut kindling, start the fire in the morning and help in the garden. Nana had vegetables and flowers out back, along with a small spring that dried up during the warmest months. I weeded on a regular basis and began to learn to be a gardener. I learned the names of everything and attended shows at the North Burnaby Horticultural

"Nana's Camp," the cottage of Bob's maternal grandmother Annie Chasteauneuf, near Dollarton on the North Shore of Burrard Inlet. Annie is seated on the railing on the left. Behind is her boyfriend, Charlie; to her right is her youngest daughter Norma, and Norma's children Janice and Dan, c. 1953. Bob Williams Collection

Society with Nana and the Chats. In those days most neighbourhoods had their own horticultural associations. It was a special treat at the end of the gardening season to visit the various neighbourhood shows across town. The most important show was at Cully's Hall, next to the drugstore at Ingleton and Hastings, where the Chats often walked off with the ribbons.

While much of the material for the cabin was hauled from the flotsam and jetsam of the inlet (there were linear islands of the stuff in the salt chuck patterned by the tidal currents), we also went up to the Dollarton sawmill just up Indian Arm. When the mill was operating, new planks and lumber would tumble into the water. We would hang around the mill like vultures waiting for the right boards to sail toward us (often aided by generous mill workers).

I would be accompanied on these expeditions by Nana's boyfriend Charlie. Charlie arrived at Nana's cabin on his days off from his job as a BC Electric Railway motorman. Transit was pretty well all streetcars or interurbans in those days, though you could take a fairly expensive coach from Dunsmuir and Seymour out to Dollarton or Deep Cove. Charlie kept a "putt-putt" boat down in Coal Harbour and headed up the inlet to camp on his regular days off. Putt-putt was the name given to the wonderful Briggs & Stratton engines that seemed to last forever. I would keep watch on the veranda in order to spot Charlie and his boat chugging under the Second Narrows Rail Bridge on the far horizon. I guess Nana was Charlie's mistress, a term I would neither have known nor understood back then. My grandmother was a very independent woman and was totally open about her relationship with Charlie, recognizing that he had a "housekeeper" at his home back in the city. What I did not know at the time was that he and his housekeeper also had a son.

Nana taught me about the garden and the various chores. Charlie taught me about the ocean and the handling of his boat and the Briggs engine. They both worked at teaching me cribbage in case their partner was ever unavailable. Come evening I would climb up on the high single bed at the far end of the living room. Nana and Charlie would have the big bed in the back bedroom. I could look out the open window and see all the way down the harbour to the big red *W* on the tower at Woodward's department store downtown. I'd fall asleep listening to the high tide sloshing under the cabin beneath me, and to the happy voices of lovers in the back room. I couldn't believe how lucky I was.

There were probably fifty shacks along the shoreline in what is now Cates Park. I never felt that it was as much of a community as Crabtown over on the Burnaby side of the inlet, though we were close with our immediate neighbours. Most of these shacks were summer homes, whereas those on the other shore were occupied year round. One of the squatters toward the point was a strange bird: a man who stumbled along the rocky beach wearing just khaki shorts and unlaced running shoes—and almost always talking to himself. I realized later that it was Malcolm Lowry, probably in a drunken reverie. Lowry was the author of *Under the Volcano*, the critically acclaimed novel that he published a few years after his shack on the beach burned to the ground. Nana made it clear: "That man is trouble, don't go near him." And I never did.

The biggest chore and challenge at camp was getting drinking water. Sometimes we went to the small general store in Dollarton owned by Mr. Cummins. Nana was always greeted warmly by the proprietor, who regularly told her she was much too young to have a grandson of my age. We would then get Mr. Cummins's permission to fill our two galvanized buckets with water from the standpipe near his small gas pump. Then we would need to pack the two buckets back to camp. The walk was well over a mile—half of it along the highway and half down the trail that my grandfather had cleared to the cabin. The buckets would be kept in the kitchen or out back, gently covered with clean linen dish towels. A ladle would hang nearby so that the water could be carefully parcelled out.

If we needed a serious supply of water, we would row the boat around the McKenzie Barge & Derrick shipyard, and pull up on the rocky shore to the west in order to access McCartney Creek. This was usually my chore. If it was low tide, it was more of a chore. The shoreline was a very rugged, boulder-strewn, barnacled mess. You had to land the boat, tuck the oars inside and pull it up from the water to avoid it drifting away when you hiked farther inland to get water that was not contaminated by the salt. All this was physically difficult in that the rocks were slimy and slippery—especially for a young boy in cheap running shoes with no tread left on the soles.

There was another cabin at the creek mouth just above high tide—unlike all of us squatters located below high tide. This cabin's occupant was an owner, not a squatter, and he took his ownership seriously. He was often out on his deck keeping an eye out for invaders. Because I wasn't very tall, I could sneak up with my two buckets and dipper to where the water was fresh. More often than not, however, the owner would notice and yell out loudly, "Get the hell off! Private property!" On being found out, I'd scramble with my two buckets over the slippery rocks, and if I didn't lose precious water in that process, I'd lose it getting the boat launched. With luck, I'd have pails three quarters full while still hearing the threats of the owner as I rowed away. I can still feel the adrenalin rush. Once the adrenalin wore off, I would feel ashamed of myself for taking this unreasonable man so seriously. Hell, I was just a ten-year-old getting drinking water for my grandma! It may have been that very scene at McCartney Creek that instilled in me a sense of social justice.

My mother was Margaret "Peggy" Emma Williams (née Chasteauneuf). She was born during the First World War on the north bank of the Fraser River in Mission, BC, which at the time was a small town. Mom's mother, Annie Bertha Chasteauneuf, was from that area too. And her mother, Margaret Sweeney, was born Margaret Lehman, the family name honoured by Mount Lehman across the river. Mom's family were true pioneers in the Fraser Valley; it's no wonder she loved the area. It's where she was born and grew up in her earlier years, and some of Mom's happiest memories as a teenager were her berry-picking summer holidays just across Hatzic Lake.

Arthur de Chasteauneuf, Mom's father, was a French immigrant from Mauritius in the Indian Ocean. When I was a small child, she told

Ringing in the New Year in 1937 with Bob's family on the Chasteauneuf and Williams sides. Bob, age four, is seated on his grandfather Chasteauneuf's lap, fourth from the left in the first row near the centre of the photo. Bob Williams Collection

me about his journey here on a sailing ship. Arthur's father, who died in 1917, is buried in the oldest part of Mission Cemetery. It's a lovely quiet spot near a ridge that looks out over the valley, just down from the segregated Japanese section of the cemetery. I remember Mom telling me her closest childhood friend was a Japanese girl who was interned or jailed in the Second World War, starting at the PNE grounds. Mom's childhood was shared with her brothers and sisters Art, Laura, Roy and Norma, mainly in North Burnaby in the Heights at 715 North Gilmore Avenue, in a house her father built when North Burnaby was just being settled with plank trails through the stumps.

My own childhood memories of that house are that it was a happy, friendly place. And grand! We lived in a very modest house, and the biggest treat for us kids was to visit our grandparents' house on Gilmore Avenue. Both my grandparents were superb gardeners. The backyard had an aviary under the pantry (full of canaries and budgies), two ponds, a waterfall and a bridge. I spent hours in the private outdoor space that they'd created. Around that house there was a deep sense of neighbourhood that was similar to the East Side neighbourhoods I had lived in both before and after. In the winter those days, I remember deep snows on the Heights and Capitol Hill, and huge bobsleds my grandfather built for the entire family.

Mom was very young when I was born—sixteen—so the responsibilities of motherhood came very early for her. A few years before she passed away in 1999, she told me how much she talked to me when I was in the womb simply because she had no one else to talk to—and how that may have explained why I was so different.

I don't know what it is about East Vancouver that captures one's loyalty. It is a rich mix of childhood friends, class consciousness, sense of place, ethnicities, local organizations, tolerance, brotherhood, camaraderie— all these things. It is home and everything that entails. It's also a village, with the many generations and associations that a village remembers. East Vancouver has both an individual and a collective history—memories that all of us share.

The East Side is "the Drive," Commercial Drive through its continuing evolution from Kay's Lunch, Hallet's Ice Cream Parlour and the Crystal Dairy in the 1940s to the Havana and Italian restaurants of today. It is Britannia Secondary School and its teachers of conscience. It is the BC Electric gas works, the wilds of False Creek Flats, Chinatown, the Still Creek ravine, the old Grandview and Olympia Theatres, the Garibaldi Club, the Rio Hall, the Co-operative Commonwealth Federation and the NDP. It's all part of the same culture and loyalties. There are roots in East Vancouver; they are my roots.

I lived most of my life in the northeast part of Vancouver and its immediate suburb of North Burnaby. My only time away from the area was in the early 1940s when my dad was stationed at the Vernon army camp in the interior of the province. In those early years our family—Mom, Dad, Fred, Marilyn and I—lived on East Twentieth Avenue just east of Nanaimo Street, beside a tiny creek that fed into Still Creek. It would be called a shack nowadays. Nearby was the Central Park tramline that traversed a trestle above Trout Lake. My parents lied about my age so that I could join the neighbourhood kids at Lord Beaconsfield Elementary School a half block away. I attended second grade at Kitchener Elementary School in North Burnaby after we moved to Union Street near Willingdon and the Acreage, which is now Willingdon Heights.

Those first years at school were magic: teachers I enjoyed, friends at school and long treks through the woods to get there. I was only five years younger than Mom's youngest sister, Norma, so I was seen much like the sixth kid in the family, meeting the same teachers my aunts and uncles had known so well. From Union Street we moved to 3970 Eton Street on the Heights, a house that is still there. Then to Vernon during the Second World War after Dad joined the Canadian Scottish Regiment, then the Royal Canadian Ordnance Corps and the Corps of Royal Canadian Electrical and Mechanical Engineers. There we lived in a three-room shack at Okanagan Landing—three rooms with no bathroom—an outhouse and a galvanized-washtub bath once a week. I found those Okanagan years of 1944–1945 almost unbearable, with the exception of summer holidays, which I spent on the coast with Nana.

When we moved back to the city in 1945, Vancouver was in the midst of a housing crisis, so we double-bunked with Nana on Gilmore Avenue. Soon though, in desperation, we moved to the back of a store at First and Nanaimo, 1657 Nanaimo Street, another building that is still there. First Avenue in those days more or less terminated at Nanaimo Street, becoming a gravel track on either side of the old Burnaby Lake tramline. It was a tough environment for a family of five, with barely a window in the place and no full bathroom. Dad built three partitions of shiplap and building paper to create a few rooms and a proper separation from the front store, which Mom operated as a children's clothing shop. We lived in that near-windowless space until 1948 when the first large veterans' housing project was built in the area now known as Renfrew Heights. It may have been home in my early teens, but I was ashamed of living in the back of a store and was unwilling to bring friends there. By that time, however, most of my life was spent outside anyway.

With my brother Fred, I joined the local Twenty-Eighth Thunderbird Scout troop, which proved to be a marvelous escape from our dismal physical environment. Hiking trips up Lynn Canyon, camping trips to the Coquitlam River, and running along log booms in the Inlet to get to our troop's sailboat were routine. We boldly clambered along logs that bridged Lynn Canyon and hiked up the mountain to Hollyburn cabins in ski season. It was pure joy. Those days led me to conclude later in life that proximity to wilderness may be *the* defining physical characteristic of life in British Columbia. For a kid living in crummy housing, the local wilderness and camaraderie of scouting friends was a godsend. Wilderness became a lifelong interest and my East Side scouting buddies became lifelong friends.

Going to school at Vancouver's venerable Britannia Secondary was a pleasure too. Commercial Drive throbbed with life at lunchtime and after school when both Britannia and the Grandview School of Commerce were in session. We teenagers provided a rush of life and

Bob Williams at around age fifteen, when he was a student at Britannia Secondary School, c. 1948. Bob Williams Collection

energy that the staid street needed. In the 1940s, Italians had not yet overtaken the working-class British immigrants who dominated the neighbourhood. I was one of the quiet kids at Britannia (Brit), unlike Dave Barrett, a guy two years ahead of me who would later become premier. My first years at high school were busy, with part-time jobs as a stock boy at Woolworth's on the Drive and at the B&B Grocery on Nanaimo Street on the weekends. After those first years at Brit, social events started taking over: school operettas, the school paper and all the scouting events.

My public education shaped me in important ways. There was only one teacher I didn't get along with at Brit—my art teacher, Mrs. Ralston—yet I still feel indebted to her. I had decided to enter an international safe-driving poster contest, but she wouldn't accept my proposal because it was late. I entered anyway, won the local contest and Canadian contest, and came in third for North America. My mother kept a small clipping in her wallet from the *Vancouver Sun* about Britannia student Bob Williams coming in third in North America in the United Commercial Travelers annual poster contest for high school students. My first newspaper clipping! My poster was completed at the last minute on the kitchen table of our one-window home at the back of 1657 Nanaimo Street. No wonder Mom was proud.

The teacher of course took much of the credit. I'm still grateful to Mrs. R. for she caused me to always, always, question authority. I also remember my English teacher, D.R. Jones, who gave me a love of English literature. When distributing our individual portraits one day, Jones held up *my* photo to show the class. I thought the photo was particularly goofy; it showed my dreamy adolescence. Jones simply said, "Isn't that beautiful?" I was embarrassed. I was lucky to have had some very good teachers who changed my life. The teachers at Brit were people of conscience; I learned later that many were active socialists. Like good teachers everywhere, they made an impact that was barely noticed at the time. Even in those days, I attended the odd CCF meeting and hung election posters on the walls of my most conservative instructors' classrooms.

Bob and his father David Williams on the roof of their home after a day's work (all without a permit) in East Vancouver, 2158 Wall Street, c. 1949. Bob Williams Collection

I didn't learn about my own political roots until I was twelve, when Mom told me that Dad, David Williams, was not my birth father. That proved to be a shock, and even more of a shock because of the circumstances at the time of the telling. As a result, for many years I felt estranged from the man I always considered to be my father. Fortunately, the estrangement did not last for too many years.

My mother told me her story of falling in love with a young man when she was fifteen or sixteen and getting pregnant. My birth father was put in jail for having "carnal knowledge" with a woman who was not his wife. They were both underage. So my birth father was put in the Edmonds jail, which was in the basement of the Burnaby City Hall. My grandfather, who served as reeve (mayor) of Burnaby at the time, presided at council meetings while his son was downstairs in jail for carnal knowledge—a charge that stalked him.

My mother ended up being a maid in my paternal grandfather's household while she was pregnant—that's the way it was in those days. She subsequently went to the Salvation Army home for unwed mothers for my birth. It was understood by the authorities that I was to be adopted, but my mother actually escaped from there with me in her arms. She got married a couple years later to my adoptive father, David Williams.

I didn't meet my birth father, Arthur Pritchard, until I was forty-two, when he was able to tell me his side of the story. Arthur said it was an early Burnaby resident, Harry Royal, the taxi owner on Capitol Hill, who bailed him out of jail. Royal advised him to get out of town. So he did, heading for California. Later, when Arthur returned to BC, my mother had already met David Williams and they were about to be married. Arthur was advised by mutual friends not to contact my mother. But what my mother was never told was that Arthur had written to her many times. Nana kept all of Arthur's letters, including the proposal letter and wedding ring that Arthur had sent from California. Only fifty years later, when Nana was on her deathbed, was my mother presented with that ring. Who knows how different our story would have been had my grandmother been honest with her daughter?

I've puzzled over the attention Nana gave me through the years, attention she sometimes denied her own children. Was I valued just because I was good at carrying out chores? I'm not sure. I do know I feel indebted to her in many ways, including for my love of the coast and the history of this place. I have Nana to thank for my love of plants, landscaping and gardening. And for my toughness and occasional stubbornness. I can really only find one explanation: my grandmother loved me. There is no greater gift.

In my later teens, I started uncovering my paternal grandfather's story. William Arthur "Bill" Pritchard joined his father in British Columbia early in the last century. The family was of Welsh heritage but had spent some time in the coal mining districts of northern England. Bill's father, James, was one of the first trade union organizers on the BC coast, organizing the coal mines in Nanaimo, in Ellensburg, Washington, and elsewhere—which in those days was an illegal occupation. My grandfather talked of involvement with his dad in that work, rowing

Bob's paternal grandfather, William Arthur Pritchard (1888–1981), was a leader of the One Big Union, serving a year in a Manitoba prison farm for seditious conspiracy in connection with the Winnipeg General Strike of 1919. He was later elected reeve (mayor) of Burnaby, BC, serving from 1930 to 1932. City of Burnaby Archives, Martha Ross. Photo ID 566-278

between coastal points to organize the workers—from Comox to Blubber Bay, with the tides against them. Workers gathered at the docks to be roused by passionate speeches encouraging them to risk their families' livelihoods in the name of worker organizations, for unions, to build a better life. It was decades later when I learned from Norman Levi that my great-grandfather was consequently wanted as a fugitive on both sides of the border.

Bill Pritchard was always active in the early trade union movement in the province. In 1919, he was sent as the BC Federation of Labour representative to the Winnipeg General Strike, a watershed event in Canadian history. The Winnipeg strike committee virtually took over local government. Like his father before him, Bill Pritchard was also sought as a fugitive from the law after the Winnipeg General strike. My own father recalled going to Calgary as a young child with his brother and mother to visit his dad. They did not realize they were being followed from the train station, but my father recalls, "We found my father in a small apartment which was full of books, and then we were busted in on by the Mounties." He also remembers "trying to bite one of the Mounties in the ass" to try to save his father from being arrested. All the books in the apartment were gathered up by the cops and taken away.

Bill Pritchard and six leaders of the strike were charged with seditious conspiracy and sentenced to jail for a year. (Another prominent socialist, J.S. Woodsworth, was also arrested on charges of seditious libel, but was not tried.) My grandfather chose not to be represented by a lawyer, instead giving his own stirring address to the jury. *W.A. Pritchard's Address to the Jury*, a history of the evolution and the building of modern freedoms for working men and women in the British Commonwealth, became a standard text for the self-taught citizens of the labour movement in this country. When he was released from jail in Winnipeg, a huge crowd came out to cheer for him, and when he returned home to the coast, another crowd showed up to greet him at the CPR station.

A decade later, my grandfather became reeve of Burnaby. I would not meet him until much later, but my sense of his time as reeve was that he was extremely creative. Burnaby was pretty rural in those days, but Capitol Hill in North Burnaby was rigid, with a grid street system over the steep hill. My grandfather was very proud of the planning job

VANCOUVER, B. C., FRIDAY MORNING, MARCH 25, 1921

Programme for Pritchard Demonstration

THE committee which has charge of the demonstration on the return of W. A. Pritchard to Vancouver has made the following arrangements:

Saturday, March the 26th—Pritchard will arrive via the C. P. R., at 9:45 a.m. All workers who are not otherwise engaged, are urged to be at the depot by 9:30 a.m.

Sunday, March the 27th—Workers parade. Parade will leave the Returned Soldiers Club (Hotel Elysium), Pender Street West, at 2 p.m., and march to the City Hall, where the South Vancouver workers will join the parade, which will then proceed to the Cambie Street grounds, where speeches will be made. Speakers: W. A. Pritchard, J. Kavanagh, Tom Richardson and Jack Harrington. The chair will be taken by W. R. Trotter promptly at 3 p.m.

Sunday evening—Three meetings, at the following theatres: Empress, Avenue and Columbia.

The arrangements at the different theatres are as follows:

Empress Theatre—Chairman, A. S. Wells. Speakers in the order named: W. A. Pritchard, J. Harrington, Mrs. Henderson.

Avenue Theatre—Chairman, J. G. Smith. Speakers: R. P. Pettipiece, W. A. Pritchard, Tom Richardson.

Columbia Theatre—Chairman, Mrs. Corse. Speakers: J. Kavanagh, Dr. Curry, W. A. Pritchard.

Monday, March the 28th—Social at the Pender Hall, corner of Pender and Howe Streets, commencing at 8 p.m. No charge for admission. Ladies are requested to bring cakes or sandwiches, and gentlemen to bring fruit. Collection to defray expenses.

In the event of the weather being unfit for a meeting on the Cambie Street grounds on Sunday afternoon, a meeting will be held in the Pender Hall.

Program for the homecoming of Bob's grandfather W.A. Pritchard, leader of the One Big Union, following his release from prison in connection with the Winnipeg General Strike. Vancouver, March 1921. *British Columbia Federationist*

he did in redesigning the roads on Capitol Hill so that they related to the topography. I of course became a planner myself long before ever meeting my father or grandfather. What do they say about blood being thicker than water?

Bill Pritchard was reeve of Burnaby in the depths of the Depression, which viciously impacted countless unemployed people in his community. Bill was determined to pay relief funds to the hungry and unemployed of his community, which was not tolerated by the provincial government. The Province removed him and his council from office, declaring the community bankrupt and placing it in receivership until the end of the Second World War.

After his removal as reeve in 1932, my grandfather was very active in the new Co-operative Commonwealth Federation (CCF) party, which was formed that year out of several labour, socialist and farmer parties. But he always felt abused by the party because of Ernie and Harold

Winch. Ernie dominated the BC party in the early days and was determined that his son Harold should own the party later on. My grandfather was interested in running for MLA in the winnable East Side ridings, but I think they gave him the university area to maintain the Winch family's control of the party. So my grandfather had hard feelings toward the CCF. But he published the *Commonwealth*, the party newspaper. My mother talked about going down to the old Holden Building on Hastings near Carrall, which had previously been Vancouver City Hall, and working with him to produce the *Commonwealth*. In the late 1930s, after Bill Pritchard joined the short-lived Social Constructive Party due to his falling out with the CCF, tragedy struck the family. A sister of my father's, Mildred, committed suicide in the basement up on Capitol Hill. Traumatized, Bill took my father and his younger brother Gilbert down to Los Angeles, where they lived for the rest of their lives.

I first made contact with Grandfather Pritchard when I was vacationing in California with a friend in the early 1970s. I found his telephone number in the Los Angeles directory and called to advise him that I was his grandson from Canada, but he indicated he had no grandson in Canada. After a little explanation, he said, "Of course," and we agreed to meet when he was next in Vancouver, which was the following year. It was then that I met Bill at his sister's apartment in Vancouver's West End, where they reminisced about early days in Burnaby. For the two of them, it was as if it were yesterday. It was both strange and comforting to be linked for a while to close relatives I'd never met before.

I met Bill several times on his trips to BC, for he loved to keep in touch with his old friends, and I learned more of his story and the real history of our region, which is our working-class history. During his time in prison after the Winnipeg strike, the conspirators liked to carry on a whole dialogue on revolution and the great utopia they wanted to create, which scared the shit out of the Canadian establishment. It was post-1917 Russia, the dawn of the Soviet Union. Bill recalled that when the group was debating vociferously, as they often did, the prison warden loved to sit and listen to these radicals talk about a better future. After a particularly heavy session, Bill recalls the jailer saying to them,

"Hell, I don't know why they sent you here on conspiracy charges. You can't agree on a damned thing!"

It was not until 1975 that I finally met my birth father, Arthur Pritchard. I was then a cabinet minister, and the busy schedule of the job allowed me to put up boundaries in order to avoid a truly emotional session with the father I'd never known. Yet it was still emotional, and provided me with my father's side of the story that had been a family secret. My wife Lea was as usual the real communicator during his visit. She was amazed at the characteristics we shared: his love of landscaping and the arts, and his involvement in liberal-left politics. I was especially fascinated by Arthur's description of the great US senate campaign between Helen Gahagan Douglas and the young, unprincipled Richard Nixon, who opportunistically labelled her a communist sympathizer in his scramble for power.

I'm sorry I did not get to know my birth father earlier. Even though I had met my grandfather several times over the years, Arthur and his wife agreed that it was typical of Bill to not mention these meetings to Arthur. It had never crossed Bill's mind that Arthur might want to meet his only child. And it's true, Bill did have a considerable ego. So I guess I come by it honestly!

While my birth father and mother's story was typical of the times, the reality was that I was part of a happy family, with a loving mom and dad, my siblings and the extended Williams and Chasteauneuf families with their own fascinating characters and histories. The Williamses lived across from Taylor Manor at Adanac and Kootenay in East Vancouver, while the Chasteauneufs lived up the hill on Gilmore Avenue in North Burnaby. The Williams household was always full of friends and family visiting the coast from Manitoba. Grandpa Williams was a successful builder who moved to Victoria to be near his second son, Ed, who was in the navy. Uncle Ed, who had been in the merchant marine before joining the navy, loved to visit us kids every time he had shore leave. My fondest memories are of when Ed was in port because he would arrive at our home with exotic gifts from faraway places. I remember coins from Treasure Island at the San Francisco World's Fair, a carved coconut head from Trinidad and shells from the South Seas. As very young children, we became aware that there was a big, exciting world out there because Uncle Ed described new aspects of it every time he came home from the sea.

When I was a teenager in 1948, we moved out of the nearly window-less building on Nanaimo Street to the luxury of a brand new home with three bedrooms and a full bathroom at the Project, as it was called in those days—Renfrew Heights, Vancouver's first veterans' housing project at 3526 Dieppe Drive. Those were happy times, though never easy financially. Mom and Dad added to the family with the birth of my brothers David and Don after our move to Dieppe Drive. After the war my dad had worked for Salmon's Transfer, but then shifted to carpentry and construction.

Mom enjoyed seeing us all grow up, making us a good home. I remember her coming home bone-tired from working as a seamstress in big sweatshops like Gault Brothers in what is now Gastown, or work-ing in the drapery business. She enjoyed that work, I think, but it wasn't easy. I think Mom knew I might have an easier life when, in about 1957, I came home with an oil painting that I'd paid $250 for, Molly Lamb Bobak's *Fog in the Subdivision*. Mom claimed I had more money than brains but reconsidered when the National Gallery contacted me six months later asking if they could borrow it from "my collection."

2. TOWN PLANNER

After high school, I ended up working at Vancouver City Hall. At the time of graduation, I hadn't really thought out my career. I worked with my dad building a house in the new Capilano Highlands development in North Vancouver. As we were finishing that project, the owner of the house said, "Hey Bob, what are you going to be doing?" When I admitted that I didn't know, he said, "I'm an assistant personnel manager at City Hall, and if you're not doing anything, come by and see me. There's always job openings at City Hall." So I went up there and was hired as an assistant in the sewer department, then as a clerk and subsequently as a draftsman. Years later, giving political speeches, I was able to quip, "I didn't start at the bottom. I started below the bottom, in the sewer department in this town."

City Hall was a world of its own. On the surface, my job was as mundane as it gets. When sewers were plugged, it was my job to get the facts and pass the information on to the outside crews. It was also my job to record all the information once the problem was cleaned up. Despite the nature of the job, understanding the context I was working within moved me along a fascinating learning curve. It was a wonderful education, and I was clearly a political student in those days. I watched the power structure from my little desk in the entry counter in the sewer department on the engineering floor.

It didn't take long to learn that the city engineer, John Oliver, was the big man in the bureaucracy, both literally and figuratively. He was the boss, and even had his own private elevator. So I started to understand status. Oliver was essentially the city manager; he made all the big decisions. But then I asked myself, "What makes *him* jump?" Here I am, an eighteen-year-old kid: "What makes the most powerful man at

City Hall jump?" What I found is there were only two agencies in this town that made him jump. One was the BC Electric Company, the old private power utility, and the other was the Canadian Pacific Railway (CPR). Anything else, he was boss. But on some of the bigger stuff, they were boss.

Then I got to know the city surveyor next door in the city survey department. We used to chum around. Hesketh Roberts was a lot older than me and really smart. His dad had been a city surveyor as well, so he had their whole databank in his head. I started getting interested in the land pattern and ownership matters, so I'd go to him and say, "Hey Hec, can you explain to me why this CPR thing is here and is like that, and then we've got this old street right of way, and yet somehow, they're winning in this game around the properties?"

And Roberts would tell me the details on how they won on that particular site and how they cheated us on this or that. He also said, "Well you know, the land title has not been settled along the shoreline."

"Really?!"

"Yeah. It's still disputed between the City, the Province and the feds in terms of who owns what."

"That's amazing."

It wasn't until many years later that it was settled. In grand tradition, the City's port got east of Main, and the CPR got west of Main. We all know where the land values are in this town. It was a classic example of deal-making at the highest levels around things that shouldn't have been subject to negotiation at all. It gave me a real understanding and appreciation of the power elite in Vancouver, and also of the property ownership structure that is critical to understanding privilege in our society.

I also learned about the pieces of the civic infrastructure. The sewer system itself was intriguing—street grades and sewer profiles, the fact that Broadway had been riddled with creeks and little ravines, property values, assessment systems, watermains, traffic counts—the myriad arcane skills that make a modern city tick. I took it all in from my vantage point at the sewer counter. At the counter I learned that Alex Sneddon, the assistant city engineer, had worked his way up from the bottom, the bottom in this case being the position of rod boy for the surveyors in the department. In turn, Sneddon liked to find untrained talent and give us a chance.

I realized that the next step up from my job was to become a draftsman. One of the draftsmen, Harry Bacon, used to do a wonderful interpretation of Sneddon's laugh and brogue. It was during one of Bacon's many comic sessions that he explained how *he* had made it up from the sewer counter to the drafting table. Bacon realized one had to be a good printer if you were to become a draftsman in those pre-computer times, so he urged me to keep fine, hand-printed records of all the unplugged sewers in the city. I continued to refine my technique until my script was very draftsmanlike. Soon, Alex Sneddon came along to check the files. Noticing the improved quality of the work, he chuckled and was clearly pleased. One month later, I was a draftsman.

Those early days at City Hall provided another kind of political awakening. Bureaucracies, turf, power structures, power elites, technologies, infrastructure—how decisions were made—were part of my daily learning. I was learning how the whole damned city was being run. One of my "fun" jobs was to measure the rain gauge on the City Hall roof. My routine morning chore was to climb up the narrow steps to the roof to check out the various rain gauges and cannisters that collected the rainfall from the previous day. Seeing Vancouver every day from the roof of City Hall, one can't help but develop an appreciation of the beauty and opportunity that comes with this place.

As I ascended to the roof, I became intrigued by the new department on the tenth floor. The planning department was then a new part of the civic administration that was invading some of the city engineers' turf, so I was curious. The planning department ended up with the tenth floor, the best view in the building. And it was all Englishmen. The City only hired planning professionals from the old country. Years later I was one of the first graduates of the planning school at UBC and had my experience at City Hall, but couldn't get re-employed as a planner because the City only hired Englishmen. Harry Bacon would often do an interpretive skit about the English planners on the tenth floor that involved sniffing snuff and tucking one's hanky under one's sleeve cuff and asking, "Hey Bob, how are things in the Foreign Office?"—where only Englishmen need apply.

After a year in the sewer department, I realized that if I wanted to do more interesting work, I'd have to go to university, something that had never been discussed as an option in our family. Despite the security of a government job, I realized it was time to take education seriously. It was a culture shock to trade Britannia Secondary—with a population of five hundred students—with UBC, which had a population of about ten thousand. My high school English teacher, D.R. Jones, had always felt I had more potential than I ever thought I did, and had he not developed in me an early love for literature, I don't think I would have managed the change. And my uncle Norman, an engineering graduate, tutored me through mathematics, a subject I'd ignored in high school. It was in second-year university that I developed an interest in economics that never left me.

When it came time for a summer job, I decided to forgo City Hall and accepted a job with the BC Forest Service. The work that summer

Bob, age nineteen, during a summer job with the BC Forest Service in Manning Park, 1952.
Bob Williams Collection

was in the West Kootenays, one of the most beautiful parts of the province. I was part of Laurie Milner's crew based in Nakusp on the Arrow Lakes. The job was to carry out a forest inventory for the region from the big bend of the Columbia River south to Castlegar. The region included places like Trout Lake City, Halcyon Hot Springs, Arrowhead, Slocan City, Sandon and St. Leon. Farther south were the old Doukhobor settlements like Krestova. The magnificent white pine forests of the Arrow Lakes, few of which exist today, were a wonder to see—the smooth silvery barrels of the trees, their exceptionally long silver-green needles and the totally clear, duff-laden understory were a grand sight for a city boy.

One of my jobs was to make food drops to various field crews throughout the region. Many of the crews were on very long hikes and needed to be able to pick up food en route rather than pack it the entire

Bob boating on Okanagan Lake during summer work with the Forest Service, sporting his first and only crew cut, c. 1953. Bob Williams Collection

length of the journey. I proved to be a quick student of air photos and getting used to stereoscopic viewing of pairs of photos so that the topography and tree types became understandable. We made the food drops by parachute from an old seaplane. The aircraft was old, even for 1952: a noisy, corrugated biplane that was a 1927 Junker with a trapdoor in the floor of the fuselage that I would lift after tying a rope around my waist, knotting the other end onto a strut in the fuselage structure. The pilot would fly in low over the site I had sized up from the air photo. I would peer over the hole in the floor unloading my parachuted food bomb.

For a city lad, all this should have been a tough adjustment, but it wasn't. Almost anything seemed possible in this new post-war era. At that time the S.S. *Minto*, an ancient CPR paddlewheeler, still plied the Arrow Lakes. The remnants of English remittance men still populated faraway corners of the lake. At Halcyon Hot Springs, a retired Boer War general came down to salute the ship when it landed. The general never failed to have his pet goat with him, tethered to his waist with heavy rope.

One of my favourite spots on the lake was Arrowhead, at the north end, south of Revelstoke. We camped near the forest service offices in Arrowhead, meeting most of the local characters. A regular there was a gnarled, deeply scarred wiry man who had been mauled by a grizzly near Trout Lake City. Our favourite cook in the valley was a tough old gal at the small local hotel and restaurant. After a hard day in the bush, Peg would put a washbasin and soap on our table and require us to wash up before we ate. Peg would make pancakes on Sundays, but her basic rule was that we eat them until she stopped cooking. For a nineteen-year-old, it was easy to live up to her requirements.

In those years, one was supposed to be twenty-one before going into a beer parlour, but all of us managed to become regulars at the spot in Nakusp we called the Gun Club, the old Leland Hotel. The livelier spot was the Saturday night dance at the community hall in Brouse, a few miles out of town. We city boys savoured it all. Our campsite near Nakusp was at the Kuskanax Creek just outside town. On weekends we'd hike to the hot springs farther up the creek. At the springs you could move wooden troughs and mix hot water with cold in the pools in the stream, setting your own temperature in the middle of the wilderness. It was Lynn Canyon writ large. We revelled in it.

In August of 1952, we were even able to get a taste of politics. The old coalition government of Liberals and Conservatives was crumbling and an election campaign was underway. One evening I slipped away from Arrowhead to a community hall up the river to attend a political rally. An unlikely group of Social Crediters had called the meeting, which had as its main speaker a preacher from Alberta. There were songs and prayers throughout, concluding with a rousing "Bringing in the Sheaves" at the conclusion. I hung in for the whole evening but concluded incorrectly that they were a group going nowhere. That group became the W.A.C. Bennett government, which remained in power for twenty years. It was even further beyond my wildest dreams on that summer evening in the Kootenays to realize I might become a key figure in removing them from office some twenty years later.

I thought forestry might be a good field to pursue because of my attraction to wilderness, but later thought better of it. The summer in the Arrow Lakes and the following summer in the Okanagan, which included hiking over the Monashee, traversing the Shuswap River from Greenbush Lake to Sugar Lake while chasing mountain goats near Mount Begbie in the old Junker, was the ultimate treat for a city boy. But other interests began to take over. Economics continued to interest me and I became proficient enough to become a tutorial instructor in Economics 200 during those undergraduate years. The group of tutorial instructors often marked second-year exams while sharing several bottles of wine. Marks for second-year students may have been a little inconsistent, but the essays probably improved with alcohol.

Leonard Marsh gave a fourth-year course in architecture that created real interest in the subject for me, and Stuart Jamieson, whose main field was labour economics, gave a couple of marvellous courses in urban sociology that completely captured my interest. Following Stu's lectures was a challenge for some students because he frequently mumbled and placed several fingers over his mouth when he was musing about ideas in a wildly random yet engaging way. But if you hung on to his chain of thought, it was like a stairway to the stars. He was the most exciting lecturer I had at UBC and I wrote my master's thesis in his field because of the scholars he introduced me to in the little-known territory of human ecology. Stuart's mother was Laura Jamieson, one of three prominent CCF women who made their mark in an earlier generation. In Laura's case she had been both an MLA and Vancouver alderman.

Architecture had always interested me, but I determined I didn't have all the talents one needs for that demanding profession. The more I looked at city planning, though, the more appealing it was, especially with my early experiences at City Hall. At this time, after the Second World War, there were a bunch of very able liberal-left people who were planning for the post-war period in Ottawa. In my fourth year of university, I met Ira Robinson, who taught in the new master's program at the UBC School of Community and Regional Planning. Robinson came from the University of Chicago, which in those days was unlike the school of today and was famous for economists like Rexford Tugwell, who pioneered radical reform in Puerto Rico. Robinson was part of a wave of former Americans emigrating to Canada to escape the McCarthy era. He was keen to have me enroll in the school. However, a year off was appealing, so I joined the Burnaby Planning Department out in Edmonds under Bill Blakely. By the following year, the Central Mortgage and Housing Corporation (now Canada Mortgage and Housing Corporation) was offering significant fellowships for postgraduates in planning. I was fortunate enough to receive that support through the subsequent two years.

The UBC planning school was a small shop in those days with no more than twenty students in the first- and second-year programs combined. Among those in the class were Darshan Johal, who became a senior UN official; Robin Sharpe, who went on to achieve fame in other ways (self-described as "the nation's most notorious child pornographer"); and Setty Pendakur, who went on to become a city alderman and professor of planning. Most students ended up working for government in various capacities. Another student in that group was Mary Rawson, a lifelong friend and future business partner. It was Rawson who introduced me to the early work of the American reformer Henry George and modern US economists who were sympathetic to his ideas, like Mason Gaffney, who then taught at the University of Wisconsin–Milwaukee.

George, the author of *Progress and Poverty*, argued that the rental value of land and resources was essentially the common property of all and should be shared by all. George favoured the taxing of that rent for public services and meeting the cost of government. He argued that taxing wages and capital had a negative impact on those factors of production, while taxing land was an incentive to put land to productive use. It was an appealing concept for a young left-winger. On further reflection, it was an appealing concept to right-wingers as well. British Columbia, a resource-rich province with a magnificent land base, seemed to me an interesting place to apply these theories. There was a growing valuable land base that was moving toward enormous growth.

Planning school times were good times. The fellowship money allowed me to travel to Europe one summer with East Side friends, and the instructors in planning and architecture all became mentors. James W. "Jim" Wilson of the Lower Mainland Regional Planning Board, who taught an excellent planning and engineering course, became a lifelong influence, and the young instructor Arthur Erickson dazzled with his design capacity. Peter Oberlander headed up the school and, when I graduated, asked me to teach there, which I did for a year. I led a special one-year planning program for Indonesian students under the Commonwealth's Colombo Plan agreement. The Indonesians were keen students who were fascinated by life in the West, even if the climate was a tad cold for them. One of the great pleasures during those days was to quietly listen to the group singing Indonesian songs in harmony outside the classroom door. However, they clammed up like crickets when they knew I was there.

My first planning job was with the Lower Mainland Regional Planning Board (which had the awkward, pre-marketing-era acronym of LMRPB). The story of the birth of LMRPB is probably one known by only a few. The person who wanted a regional planning board the most was Tom McDonald, who was the executive director of the local branch of the Community Planning Association of Canada (CPAC). McDonald was a big man in both the obvious and best senses of the word, and had one of the best speaking voices I've ever heard.

McDonald was an idealistic Red Tory and seemed to favour me as this young, radical graduate. I was just out of school and he made me the chair of CPAC's Vancouver branch. McDonald worked out of a couple of small offices in the Vancouver Block near Georgia and Granville. You would hear his booming voice working the telephone on the issues of the day, echoing down the hall as you approached his office. Over one of our regular lunch meetings at the Seymour Room cafeteria of the nearby Hudson's Bay store, McDonald told me how he got a regional planning board established.

I believe it was probably in 1951, when the governing coalition government in Victoria was falling apart. Premier John Hart had been replaced by Byron Johnson, and the Liberals and Tories in the coalition were sniping at one another. Once again liquor licensing and the attorney general's office had a distinct odour about them and the warring factions were dividing the spoils. For many of the soon-to-be departing politicos, it was a time to grab a chunk of Crown land, some beautiful waterfront, for a pittance. And for some of our corporate elite, it was a time to convert leases into indefeasible title. As a straight-arrow prairie Tory, Tom McDonald was offered his chunk of the spoils in British Columbia. Tom being Tom, however, asked for only one thing, and of course it was not for himself. McDonald asked for a statute to create the Lower Mainland Regional Planning Board, and he got it. As I've said on other occasions, the birth of regional planning in British Columbia was not an immaculate conception.

The Lower Mainland Regional Planning Board was located on Columbia Street in New Westminster, which in those days was the main street for Surrey and the Fraser Valley. A small group of dedicated planners led by Jim Wilson pioneered the idea of a more carefully thought out development approach to the new suburbs, which were expanding rapidly after the resettlement of veterans of the Second World War. The most senior planner on Jim Wilson's staff was A.D. (Alistair) Crerar, who became my lifelong friend and mentor.

The first project Crerar had of some scale was the Industrial Survey of the Lower Mainland. A handful of university students were hired for the summer to work on the survey. The team included Crerar, Mary Rawson, P.D. McGovern and me. The purpose of the survey was to interview most of the industrial employers in the region to see what made us collectively tick. What were they producing? Where did they get their supplies? Who did they employ? What was their payroll? What was the future? It was an interesting exercise, and for much of the summer we worked out of Vancouver City Hall, familiar territory for me. I covered a range of heavy industries such as foundries and machine works. But I also had the junkyards, and often the owners were only a cut above the junkyard dogs that covered the graveyard shift. But I persevered and began to understand the salvage and junk business. Many years later, Crerar told me that I was the only one able to handle that tough assignment. "It's a dirty job, and somebody has to do it." Was that to be my motto later, in the political world?

At the end of the summer there was a back-to-school party up in Royal Heights for the departing cadre of summer employees at the LMRPB. For me, an East Side boy, it was a sense of arrival. Planning was the field I wanted to devote a good chunk of my life to, and I'd found a worthy mentor in Crerar. The board, and Crerar in particular, carried out work that was unequalled in the country. Crerar's seminal work on urban sprawl in Surrey was noticed across the continent. Subsequently, he was invited to head up the long-range planning role in the City of Toronto, where he again pioneered work, such as transportation demand management, which was a good twenty years ahead of its time. At the same time, the best neighbourhood planning activity was taking place in Toronto.

During this period, Crerar was becoming more and more interested in bigger economic questions, as was I. He moved on to work with the Atlantic Development Board at a senior level under Allan J.

MacEachen, an important federal cabinet minister of that era. I, in turn, had become more interested in the provincial economy at home, and the nature of the resource industries of BC. Much later, Crerar came home and headed up an agency of cabinet when the NDP took power, which we called the Environment and Land Use Committee (ELUC) secretariat, implementing the Agricultural Land Reserve and countless other projects. Some of us considered the work of Crerar and his team to be the best on the continent, setting a new standard that made it possible some twenty years later to begin their work anew under Commissioner Stephen Owen and Deputy Commissioner Denis O'Gorman in the Harcourt government, leading conflict resolution teams to resolve resource and land-use conflict through the Commission on Resources and Environment (CORE).

Norman Pearson was another critical player on the staff of the LMRPB. Pearson has never been recognized for being the father of the regional parks system for Greater Vancouver and the Fraser Valley. Today it's a huge success. Pearson was always an activist. From the LMRPB, Pearson was probably the key influence in preventing the new Lions Gate Bridge from requiring a freeway though the city by presenting better alternatives. As mayor at that time, Mike Harcourt can take much of the credit for stopping it, but Pearson was one of the coterie of others that made the big difference. So it's wonderful fun that Pearson and I later created the Seabus service during our administration to replace the function of the proposed bridge in the quickly evolving regional transportation network in Greater Vancouver.

At the LMRPB we planned and plotted together on diverse projects—particularly the Official Regional Plan for the Lower Mainland. It all came to a head later when the board was very active in seeking to relocate the railway to Roberts Bank. I was the young pup that had just been elected an NDP MLA, and I appeared in my LMRPB capacity before W.A.C. Bennett in his cabinet room. At the time, being an MLA was considered a part-time job with part-time pay, so many of us had day jobs. As a result of that meeting, the government decided they wanted to get rid of this bloody regional planning agency that was trouble for them. A province-wide "regional district" system got created as a way to break the LMRPB into three parts. The goal was to destroy the LMRPB and the troublesome planners there, and break up the well-directed political power that the board represented.

After I taught in the UBC planning school for a year, there was an opening for a significant new planning job in the region, which Jim Wilson urged me to apply for. The municipality of Delta was ready to hire their first director of planning. Delta at that time was outside the Vancouver suburban orbit in that the mainland access from Vancouver was through New Westminster and the Pattullo Bridge. Even in those days, travel time from Delta was well over an hour. There was a small ferry-boat service at Woodwards Landing that linked Ladner and Richmond.

The provincial government had decided to replace the ferry with what is now the George Massey Tunnel at Deas Island, reducing the travel time to Delta to twenty-five minutes. The tunnel represented enormous change for the community and a giant increase in land values. This was to be an on-the-ground education in Henry George's urban economics. Infrastructure that would change travel time to downtown Vancouver produced massively higher land values for landowners who had contributed nothing themselves. As some Georgist economists would argue, they made money in their sleep.

Delta then, as now, was essentially three or four different communities. First, there were the farmers on the fertile lowlands stretching from Surrey to Westham and Reifel islands, along with the little village and service centre of Ladner. Then there was the upland area of North Delta, rapidly suburbanizing on the edge of Surrey below Scott Road. To the south was Tsawwassen and the uplands above Beach Grove, attached to Point Roberts. A distinct community existed along the river, comprised mainly of families tied to the fishing industry. Overall, it was a community that had changed very little throughout the century, with the exception of North Delta, a fast-growing suburb adjacent to Surrey. Ladner and the farmlands were a very cohesive community. South Delta was sparsely settled but was a land promoter's dream with its low rainfall, undeveloped uplands and beautiful beaches. The developers and speculators were all there ready to carve up the old large holdings, flip the land quickly and get out.

After my academic years it was an enormous culture shift to take on the Delta assignment. Delta's municipal council was an interesting mix and quite representative of the community. The mayor of my first council was John Kirkland, a retired farmer who had done well subdividing his land and was close to the small professional establishment in the village of Ladner. The chair of the planning committee of the council was Alvin Bastedo, a Ladner optometrist who lived in North Delta. Bastedo was an irreverent Red Tory who had a quick mind and wit that often got him in trouble. He was a pleasure to work with. Erwin Huesken from North Delta was an active fundamentalist who saw most issues in a very narrow context. Part of the fishing-labour community was Alderman Carl Liden, who boldly supported most of the planning initiatives. Harold Savage, from one of the oldest farm families, was a strong influence amongst the council members.

Kirkland was soon replaced as mayor by Clarence Taylor, who owned a radio and TV repair shop in Ladner. All this proved to be a volatile mix for a young man just out of planning school and determined to do as good a job as he could. Clarence Taylor was intrigued by and supportive of me. He even pointed to his earlier left-wing views and support for an early CCF leader who made a great name for himself on radio, Lyle Telford, an MLA and Vancouver mayor who everyone listened to in the late 1930s. But Taylor was very much a part of Ladner, and Ladner was nothing if it wasn't conservative and self-interested.

For a young planner, Delta was a feast. I had been well prepared by my mentors at the Lower Mainland Regional Planning Board, particularly Jim Wilson and Alistair Crerar. Getting to know Crerar in many ways was better than going to planning school. Working on the industrial land survey gave us a real understanding of how the Lower Mainland literally worked. I didn't know it at the time, but I got the toughest assignments that summer. Crerar's research in those days were landmark studies that even made Ontario take notice: the

Industrial Survey of the Lower Mainland, as well as his earlier survey of urban sprawl, a term Crerar himself coined for the spreading land-use mess in Surrey.

Partly as a result of Crerar's mentorship, I undertook my own look at urban sprawl in Delta, primarily in Ladner, the farmlands and South Delta and Tsawwassen. The report I issued caused quite a stir at the time. Drawings in that report showed premature subdivision in Tsawwassen devoid of real development, leaving behind a huge maintenance bill for the municipality. I recommended a substantial rezoning program to limit the residential zoning and roll back some lands into farmland status again. (This was prior to the Agricultural Land Reserve—more on that later.) There were huge public hearings over the issue, with hundreds of people coming out to be heard. At the time I didn't think much about the stir I was creating, I just thought it was what I should do if I was serious about planning.

We were able to move on saving more of the farmland in Delta. Indeed, even Alderman Harold Savage's farm was rezoned back to farmland. I suspect it suited him in that he probably pocketed the developer's down payment and kept the farm to boot. While Savage certainly viewed much of the stuff I was saying as socialist nonsense, I'm pleased he had the courage in later years to reflect positively on how prescient many of my concerns and ideas were.

My office during my hectic days in Delta was in the attic of the old municipal hall, which is now the city museum in the heart of Ladner. It had been the caretaker's residence in the old building, so I helped move the bedspring out before I started my duties as planner. It was that kind of place. The old guard in the civic bureaucracy—the city clerk, the comptroller and some senior engineering staff—liked the old ways of the "family compact" that had governed Delta for decades. But times were changing, and fast. I was part of a new breed at City Hall, along with the new city engineer, Ron Taylor, and the new city solicitor, Clive Nylander.

The superintendent of works, Vern Wiedmann, was an old hand who found the new breed to his liking. Taylor was a super engineer, well schooled and thoughtful. He was impressed with the work I was doing and wanted to complement and support it. My candle, however, was probably burning a little too strongly for the overt politicians around the council table, and a short term for me might mean the same for my colleagues who were too supportive. It turned out that was the way it was to be, but not before getting a lot of work done. I was sounding off on every conceivable issue, such as:

- urban sprawl;
- saving farmland;
- enhancing the Ladner village;
- creating Ladner Harbour Park;
- acquiring dyke water frontage by Swenson's farm;
- developing Centennial Beach;
- saving Boundary Bay from developers for wildlife;
- creating public pathways along the waterfront; and
- relocating the Tsawwassen Causeway road.

Through it all, Alvin Bastedo and Carl Liden were the aldermen (the title for councillors prior to 1993) who supported me consistently. Bastedo was a Red Tory and the logic of the planning arguments appealed to him. More than that, he probably just admired the gutsiness I showed through all these small-town battles. Carl Liden, in turn, saw it all as a social democratic agenda. It was the first of many times when I saw that wonderful junction where right meets left and the differences are not very great.

While I may have been a political burden for Bastedo to carry into the next civic election, his own quick wit was probably his ultimate undoing. At a public hearing centring on a proposed rezoning in North Delta, a fair crowd had assembled to consider a new neighbourhood commercial zone in the heart of the community. It was a relatively modest proposal that I, as planner, had endorsed. One woman, a local resident, was very opposed to the idea, saying the change would create more traffic and this would be a safety hazard. Bastedo couldn't resist prodding the woman: "What makes you an expert on safety, madam?" The woman responded, "Well, I have six kids, so that's how I know."

Bastedo could simply not resist spitting out his one-liner: "Lady, if you have six kids, you sure can't call yourself an expert on safety!" The rejoinder brought the house down, but Bastedo was not re-elected.

The agenda that I put before council was a demanding one for any group. Delta was bound to run into trouble simply because the interest groups that coalesced around the land rush were too powerful. There were the professionals in Ladner—like the big law firm headed by Herb Ivens and his brother. There were land surveyors like Cliff Matson who were doing too well keeping things as is. And there were local realtors like Ted Towers and George Hodgins who had too much to gain. Hodgins, the most active realtor in Tsawwassen, had married Harold Savage's youngest daughter. There were the engineering and construction folks who had an interest in the land boom. Most of all, there were the landowners, farmers, investors and speculators who had never seen such a quick return in their lives. The growing interest of all these players could not, in the end, be ignored by politicians who wanted to continue getting elected. Suzanne Westphal, the columnist for the *Delta Optimist*, couldn't resist the temptation of regularly aiming at the easy target of the first planner in Delta. Once Alvin Bastedo was defeated, I should have realized I would move up on the hit list.

But it never really crossed my mind. After all, I was working long hours churning out pithy reports on every imaginable subject. Furthermore, at the height of the agricultural land fight, I received threats on my life from unsavoury eastern promoters who had made their way to Delta. I was working for the public interest; therefore, I was naively confident I would survive. And I thought I had the mayor on my side. But other forces were at work on the mayor.

My time in Delta was an exciting departure from the academic world, putting me in touch with the players, both good and bad, who ran the system. Friends of mine in recent years have said there are only one hundred real decision-makers in Vancouver. One can argue with the delineation, but there's little doubt that we're not talking big numbers. Despite this, it's also true that people—individuals—can make a big difference if they truly want to.

There's always a secondary level of player too, folks who care and are always chipping in at critical times, leveraging the limited power they hold. Sometimes these players are bureaucrats who care. Art Benson comes to mind as an example: a biologist with the Canadian Wildlife Service who was passionate about the importance of Boundary Bay for waterfowl as well as its role in the west coast flyway for migratory birds. Benson played a critical role in saving Boundary Bay from developers.

Some downtown folks were players in Delta. Percy Burr of Pemberton Realty, one of the big downtown firms, had an impact on industrial zoning along the river and on Tilbury Island. Percy had farmer roots going for him as well, with family members continuing to farm the delta. Leonard Boultbee of another big downtown real estate firm, Boultbee Sweet, had links with Delta residents and was keen on getting control of Boundary Bay for an enormous dredge-and-fill development. The bay is an enormous tidal-water sandbar stretching from Blaine to Point Roberts, Washington, encompassing an area about ten miles wide and three or four miles deep. Boultbee envisioned a port with industrial and commercial development, along with hundreds of channels of water created by dredging the sandbar to create thousands of new waterfront lots.

There was space in Boundary Bay for a huge new city and tens of miles of new waterfront. Today that all seems a little fanciful, but the world of the 1960s was far less burdened with process than the world of today. For me it was a big, tough job to sideline Boultbee, though his own arrogance helped, as did the constant leveraging of Art Benson. The same Art Benson subsequently worked on the Canada Land Inventory, providing the land-quality database that was critically needed for the Agricultural Land Reserve brought in by the province's first NDP government in 1973.

I have always been keen about parkland preservation and as a planner was able to increase Delta's parkland base. The main addition during my tenure was the establishment of Ladner Marsh as a large municipal park. In that case, it was possible to convince wildlife biologists to back away from the key land areas near Ladner in order to establish a large riverfront park with waterfront on both Ladner Slough and along the south arm of the Fraser River. Working with the same biologists on the preservation of Boundary Bay probably didn't hurt in achieving the trade-off on Ladner Marsh, a lesson that helped in later years.

Another set of toes I stepped on in Delta belonged to A.E. "Dal" Grauer, the former boss of the BC Electric Company. Grauer came from Richmond farm elite and owned a large farm on the north side of Beach Grove along Boundary Bay. The Province planned the new highway from the Deas Island Tunnel to the Tsawwassen Causeway. The alignment proposed was a mile north of the Tsawwassen hillside or escarpment. I felt it was better to shift the alignment south to the base of the escarpment in order to avoid sprawl on the intervening farmland. Grauer met me in my dinky attic office where I tried to explain my reasoning. He would have none of it. After all, my proposal would carve through *his* farmland. "Damned if I'll let you bugger up my children's inheritance," he declared. As it turned out, Delta City Hall was no different than Vancouver City Hall. When the BC Electric came calling, the BC Electric won.

The straw that broke the camel's back for the Delta council was my role as subdivision approving officer. The approving officer for land subdivisions is appointed by the local council but has authority and responsibility under a provincial statute. I therefore saw that role as independent of council, a purist view I might not agree with nowadays after a long political career. I got into a little trouble with a subdivision proposed for English Bluff Road near the US border. That part of the bluff was very unstable. Indeed, the bluff on the adjoining property had sloughed off and buried two summer homes on Tsawwassen Beach below some years earlier. I refused to approve subdivision of the adjacent lands into upland and lowland parcels due to it "not being in the public interest" in view of the vulnerability and instability of the site. The case went to provincial court, and I lost. The judge in the case claimed I was being "too paternalistic."

A little later, during my final days as approving officer in Delta, I asked for waterfront pathway dedications along both Tsawwassen

Beach and Cohilukthan Slough in Ladner, so that at a later stage the public could walk unimpeded along these waterways. The precedent, in fact, had been established in Beach Grove, which had a dedicated ten-foot pathway along the adjacent shoreline in Boundary Bay. These requirements proved too much for the municipal council, for after an in-camera meeting, Mayor Clarence Taylor asked for my resignation. The alderman who had replaced Alvin Bastedo, Henry Thomas, who lacked Bastedo's wit and capacity, was keen to see me go and had convinced the majority of council. Taylor seemed sheepish when he advised me of the decision. Sheepish, but relieved. The relief was, I think, short-lived, for then the council created a new majority around a range of other issues that Taylor was not always happy with. The local elite—the family compact, the historic governors of Delta—were in full control again.

Vern Wiedmann was a wonderful, hard-working, hard-driving and probably hard-drinking character who I met and grew to love when I was in Delta. We cared for and admired each other—first and foremost because there was no bullshit between us; we truly told it as it was. Wiedmann headed up public works in Delta. He used to come up to my office to josh with my secretary Marilyn Dunbar and draftsman assistant Tom Dennison. But he came up primarily to talk seriously with me, and we exposed our practical left views of the world to each other. One of my greatest regrets was that I missed Wiedmann's funeral because it was in the middle of an election I was involved in.

Wiedmann and his wife Ilene would come to my huge parties on 2158 Wall Street—Boxing Day was my big party of the year. All my friends and buddies from over the years would arrive up those rickety back steps into the upstairs unit my dad and I had illegally transformed into a spacious pad. It opened up to the harbour looking toward the Lions Gate Bridge and the working docks nearby. Mary Rawson would be there, and her late dear friend Mary Mackenzie, and all of my East Side buddies—Ray Holmes, Bill Boutilier (a part-time roommate), Ron and Larry Doyle, Bill Hammond, Jim Wilson, Dave O'Brien (from planning circles), NDP

View of Burrard Inlet from Bob's porch at 2158 Wall Street, Vancouver, c. 1965. Bob Williams Collection

workers Don and Dana Fraser, and others such as Vern Wiedmann, Ilene and my future wife, Lea.

Wiedmann was a careful observer. He listened. He overheard. He was his own intelligence agency. And he was my protector. Wiedmann could spot a phony a mile away. At the end of the Wall Street parties, he would brief me on who at the event were my real friends. He was always prescient and wanted me to survive in the long run. And then, when we were into our last drink before he went home (and everyone else already had), he'd say, "You know, Bob, you're so advanced from your political colleagues, they don't even come close." He was dead serious.

3. JOINING THE CCF

My friend Mary Rawson had been a staunch Tory, a fact I didn't know at the time. Back at that stage I would have thought "progressive conservative" was an oxymoron, but we all move on. Rawson was a Red Tory. As a student in the master's program with me, she listened to my regular grousing about the politics of the day and felt I should quit being a complainer and use my energy in a positive way. It was after attending a "Follow John" Diefenbaker rally that I told Rawson I saw Dief as a demagogue. Rawson then urged me to join the party of my choice, which of course was the Co-operative Commonwealth Federation. Rawson convinced me that this was indeed what any caring citizen should do. Her own views were not a consideration. That was 1957, more than sixty years ago.

The Co-operative Commonwealth Federation, or CCF as it was generally known, had offices in what was then the Holden Building on the south side of Hastings Street just east of Carrall. I proceeded to the Holden Building, rode the rickety elevator up six floors and joined the party. I rightly considered it a serious move at the time, but little did I realize how momentous a choice I had made. When I reflect on the name of the party, I find it overflows with meaning. Co-operation was important back then, just as I believe it needs to be today. The Commonwealth question—our land, resources and people—a common wealth indeed. And a federation of like-minded people and groups. For me it still has resonance, unlike the labels of today.

After joining the CCF, I became an active member in my own constituency of Vancouver East, getting involved in the local governance of the riding association, drafting resolutions for conventions and attending all the meetings. Most of our meetings took place at the old

Rio Hall, an early meeting and dance hall that was actually owned by the constituency association. That in itself was a lesson. Old-timers like Annie McGougan and her husband literally saved pennies to buy that hall in the depth of the Depression as a base from which to convey their cause to the community. Talk about results. To this day, some three or four generations later, most of the East Side supports the NDP.

Those old folks were strong and generally came from the old country, namely England and Scotland. As former provincial leader Bob Strachan once said at a meeting at Rio Hall, "Vancouver East is like Scotland. When Carlyle was asked in the Highlands what they produced on these barren lands, he replied, 'Men. We produce men on these lands.'" So it was with our membership in those days, but not only with men. We had a women's auxiliary that made most of the money and looked after Rio Hall. They were an astute group. They created a social club with a bingo licence, and they had rummage sales, bake sales, potluck dinners and Christmas benefits. They were there in body, spirit and brains, providing most of the funds for elections.

There was Edna Nicols who never missed a meeting, chewing away on false teeth that were a little too loose. Lil Winterford was always there ready to support any new fundraising activity and involve her many relatives. Lil's brother Happy was always available to play Santa at the Christmas benefit. Hazel Nielson along with her husband, Jim, was always about, keeping the membership rolls up to date. Mrs. Macdonald with her big treed lot was always available for a summer garden party. Women like Annie McGougan often had the veto at regular meetings. McGougan never wasted time and never minced words. She usually brought her knitting to our lengthy executive meetings, and never said very much, but when she said no, that was it.

The men contributed almost equally, in their own way. Sam Lake, who lived in a basement suite on Grant Street, wore running shoes long before they became fashionable, and always made himself available for delivering pamphlets or working on the sign crew. Marie Apostoluk, who loved working with the old guys, was always available as the boss of the sign crew. And Apostoluk, while sharing some manly qualities, kept letting the sign crew and everyone else know that she was *all woman*, especially after the death of her husband, Henry. Henry, who had been blinded in a mining accident, had worked at a Canadian National Institute for the Blind kiosk that I had helped at.

Frank O'Dowd was a quiet, committed activist who was always looking for new talent in the riding. O'Dowd encouraged me to draft motions and policy resolutions for provincial conventions. I drafted a motion supporting the idea of municipal industrial estates—city development of new sites for manufacturing and industry. The Brits had been doing it for years, as had most Europeans. When I made the motion to put it forward to the convention, I was challenged by one of the big names in the riding, Harold Thayer, who was provincial secretary of the party. He argued we had to be careful about putting forth too many leftist ideas, that "people would think we wanted to own their very toothbrush."

Unaccustomed as I was to political rhetoric, I was flabbergasted by the nonsense coming out of Thayer. A member none other than Grace MacInnis, the daughter of CCF founder J.S. Woodsworth, immediately challenged Thayer, arguing that we must be open to new ideas. "And this is a new idea that makes sense to me," she said. With Grace's support, the motion passed with a huge majority. I subsequently attended my first provincial convention (1957 or 1958), which was of such a small scale that it actually took place in the Mount Pleasant Legion Hall at Eleventh and Main. The motion supporting municipal industrial estates passed easily. My first big initiation into provincial politics was complete.

One of the pillars of Vancouver East CCF politics was Harry Whelan. Whelan was a good old boy, an insider who was very close to Harold Winch, the MP for the riding. Winch had also been the leader of the opposition in Victoria from the days when he and his father, Ernest, shared seats on the opposition benches. Harry Whelan had been Winch's buddy through the years, and once he got to know you, would regale you with Depression-era stories of scrambling to find a white shirt and tie for Winch to wear at big political rallies. More than that,

3. JOINING THE CCF

Winch had a serious drinking problem and Whelan was often the guy who had to splash cold water on Winch's face, keep him walking with black coffee, dress him in the white shirt, and push him up on stage, hoping it would work one more time and knowing from experience that it would. Indeed, Harold Winch in his prime could perform political oratory that would both convince and excite the crowds, leaving them cheering.

Harry Whelan and the younger movers and shakers in the riding would retire to the Collingwood Legion a block away to discuss the evening's constituency or executive meeting and to plan strategy for the next. I was invited to the Legion by Whelan soon after I became active. Later on, younger members like Stu Headley were regulars around the Legion tables. Those sessions usually didn't include the members of the women's auxiliary.

Later, when I was a city councillor in Vancouver, one of the aldermen, Halford Wilson, told me that the first city council he was part of in the 1930s operated in a similar manner. In those days, the Holden Building on East Hastings was in fact the City Hall. Wilson said that once the official council meeting was over, they would retire to the Dodson Hotel beer parlour across the street to determine the fate of the *next* week's council resolutions over a beer. The important council meetings were, of course, the unofficial ones across the street in the beer parlour.

Harry Whelan was also close to Arthur Turner, the long-time MLA for Vancouver East. Indeed, Turner had represented our area for over twenty-five years and unbeknownst to me was fairly keen to retire. But Turner would not retire until he was satisfied about his replacement. The president of the riding association was Stu Hodgson, a member of the International Woodworkers of America (IWA) executive. Hodgson was an outgoing, gregarious individual who could speechify on whatever was required of him. Hodgson was ambitious and saw the MLA job as his. But neither Harry Whelan nor Arthur Turner were happy with the prospect of Hodgson becoming MLA and they were determined that it would not happen. Turner was looking for commitment and depth, qualities he did not see in Hodgson.

As it turned out, luck was with Hodgson. After he gave up the presidency of the riding to me, he publicly renewed his friendship with Arthur Laing, who was the Liberal MP for Vancouver South and minister of northern affairs. In those days there were many sawmills in South Vancouver along the Fraser River, and an ambitious IWA member could be helpful to an MP with a future. The benefits of course turned out to be mutual. Several years later, in 1967, Hodgson ended up becoming the first commissioner of the Northwest Territories under Laing. He must have felt like he'd died and gone to heaven, ruling almost as a monarch in the North. He even got to bust open a crock of gin to share privately with the young Prince Charles when he toured the area. For Arthur Turner, Stu Hodgson's move confirmed an uneasiness that he'd always felt.

Grace MacInnis was nursing her ill husband, Angus, who for decades had been the Vancouver East MP. A trade unionist, Angus MacInnis had been a leader in the Street Railwaymen's Union (from the old BC Electric streetcar system). After Angus's death, Grace MacInnis was able to spend more time on constituency matters and proved to be a mentor. She saw me as an up-and-comer and supported me in almost everything I did. MacInnis showed me the longshoreman's hook in her study from the days when her slightly built father had to work on the Vancouver waterfront to support his family. She also told me about her and Harold Winch having to share boots to go to school when both their families were in Gibsons Landing.

It was MacInnis and old-timers like Nazar Patan who told me about dirty tricks played by the local communists in the 1930s. MacInnis recalled an early CCF rally at the Beacon Theatre wrecked by communists marching in with their red banners unfurled. Patan, who himself had been a member of the Communist Party in the 1930s, told me that they had asked him to spy on the CCF, but he proved to be inept at the job. "The CCFers made so much more sense than the communists," Patan said, "that I quit the communists right away."

In those first years I was still learning, both at university and in the riding. I was a little shy, and certainly not aggressive. Folks like Harry

3. JOINING THE CCF

Whelan wondered, I'm sure, if I could ever make the grade as a provincial politician. I was in my early twenties then, with a heavy course load in graduate studies and an active social life with my East Side buddies like Ray Holmes, Bill Hammond, Ron Doyle, Holger Ostman and Dick Ion. Six of us owned a cabin on Hollyburn Ridge; I've often said that I don't think I could have made it through university had we not had the cabin up the mountain. We'd head up the mountain on Friday night, often with a five-dollar forty-ounce bottle of wine in our parka: Bon wine, as I recall, a product of the long-defunct Saanich winery of the attorney general of the day, Herbert Anscomb.

That yellow cedar cabin on Hollyburn was called Ski Heil! and everything in it had been packed up the mountain on people's backs, including an enormous 1920s cast iron stove, complete with warming oven up above. I had noticed the place in the want ads of the *Sun*. The price was $300, a princely sum of $50 each. Kids from the East Side with their own mountain resort for fifty dollars each! It was the best real estate investment any of us ever made. It slept eight or a dozen, depending on the circumstances.

We got to know the whole mountain crowd: Oscar, the Norwegian who ran the lift at Hi-View Lodge, Harry and Fred Burfield at Hollyburn Lodge at First Lake, and of course Norm Deacon at Westlake Lodge. There were dances every Saturday night at the Westlake Lodge that everyone on the hill attended. It was there that we all finished our forty-ounce "porch climber." My buddies didn't share my interest in politics to any great extent, but they were East Siders, and it was a given that East Siders supported the CCF.

Back at Vancouver East, it became more and more apparent that it was a watershed time in the riding's affairs. Arthur Turner was ready to retire after his last election in 1963, but had to be satisfied about his replacement. Others outside the riding were sensing the opportunity to represent the safest seat in the province for what was now known as the New Democratic Party. There was a young lawyer in town who was getting noticed, speaking out at Victory Square and public meetings—Tom Berger. Berger of course went on to have a superb career as a lawyer and royal commissioner on the Mackenzie River Pipeline, and brief forays as a MP, MLA and provincial Supreme Court judge.

However, he and his envoys who were sent to test the political waters at the Rio Hall found a cool response. The classic east–west battle lines of class in the city were as strong as ever in the 1960s. Berger deserved a warm welcoming committee; he was immensely capable, a superb lawyer and a champion of civil liberties and Indigenous rights. What Tom Berger's colleagues had not figured on was the class consciousness that was still pervasive on the East Side. Beyond all that, however, more and more people had come to see me as the likely candidate for the next election (which turned out to be in 1966)—especially after Harry Whelan and Arthur Turner had attended my big public hearings in Delta—all of which I was unaware of. And, the key player in the riding, the Scottish elder in the back corner tending her knitting, had made up her mind much earlier. (I was not aware of that either.) So when Tom Berger's name was mentioned at one of our executive meetings, it got a quick, terse no from Annie McGougan. McGougan used her veto, and Tom Berger's envoys focused instead on the riding of Vancouver–Burrard.

In so many ways, the riding of Vancouver East was a village with countless networks, a village that was very proud of its members in Ottawa and Victoria. One event above all remained in the minds and memories of people on the East Side: the post office police riot of the 1930s. Unemployed men rallied in downtown Vancouver and occupied the central post office at Granville and Hastings. Mayor Gerry McGeer called police to forcibly break up the occupation. The police ruthlessly beat the workers with billy clubs. Many were injured and the people of the East Side were in shock over the aggressive acts of the police. All these men wanted was work, and to be able to look after their families. The pacifist hero of the post office occupation was Harold Winch, a young, unemployed electrician, who was beaten more harshly than anyone.

The East Side, generations later, never forgot. Winch was a hero. He was family. We were always proud of him; he was ours. I always felt that having the privilege of being part of this community and this history meant I had a special obligation—that I must try and come close to the achievements of those who had gone before. We were proud of Harold and Ernest Winch, but we understood that Harold, while one of the grand orators of his day, still didn't have the depth and compassion of his father. Ernest was also a father who was too ambitious for his son, creating a burden that was too much to bear. We understood that Harold had to escape into alcohol. It was a family secret—a family secret shared by a quarter of the city.

We also celebrated the brilliance and compassion of the other leaders in the CCF and NDP. Grace MacInnis was radiant when she walked into a room. Like her mother Lucy, Grace was a university graduate. Lucy was one of the first women in Canada to graduate from McGill, while Grace graduated from the Sorbonne in Paris. Other compassionate leaders like Arnold Webster were known for their fine work in the public schools. Webster was principal of Grandview High School of Commerce at First and Commercial Drive, where he improved the lives of all the kids he came into contact with—especially those from Chinatown. Visiting MLAs and speakers were celebrated. Colin Cameron, the MLA and MP from Vancouver Island, spoke about the resource industries with a depth of knowledge few others in the province shared. And many lawyers, such as Frank Mackenzie, made a difference in those early days. All this the village knew and appreciated.

4. VANCOUVER ALDERMAN

The sense of injustice that was common on the East Side when I was a young man kept boiling up. In so many ways we were the forgotten part of the city, and I felt a breakthrough could be made. Mary Rawson had urged me to become active in politics, and surprisingly—in view of future loyalties—Alex Macdonald's wife, Dorothy, also urged me to become active in civic politics. But it was urging I did not need, for after a few years in community planning circles and appearing regularly in city council, I was more than convinced that City Hall needed to be shaken up. The time seemed right in the fall of 1964.

As president of the Vancouver East NDP provincial constituency association, I talked up the possibility of my candidacy at our monthly meetings. Everyone was in favour. That meant we had the makings of a campaign committee, a sign committee and a workforce to canvass, or at least deliver pamphlets, from that group alone. Beyond that, all of my East Side buddies, former Rover Scouts and other friends were keen to provide support. No one in those days had used lawn signs in a civic campaign and I felt it would provide a certain recognition or name association that could help us break through.

A small group of disgruntled folks, most of whom were not NDPers, had the desire to tackle the Non-Partisan Association (NPA), the governing civic party. I saw this anti-NPA slate as an opportunity to broaden my supportive base, so I sought and obtained their support. It was a completely crass decision and I never once planned on being committed to the slate, other than in the broad sense that they were better than the NPA. My plan was to be an East Side candidate, but one with professional skills; I was the first town planner to run for council. My plan was also to use as much of the traditional NDP organization as I could, and that too made a difference.

I'd been a "soldier" for several years, so I knew who to tap for work. The best volunteer silk-screen sign maker was a wonderful middle-aged working man who I'd got to do the signs for one of Harold Winch's campaigns. He lived in a room in Mount Pleasant, literally cutting the screen while sitting on his cot. I'd developed the slogan for Winch: "Worker for the People" (a different era indeed). Our campaign slogan was simpler and a little less left. In red and white, the message was "Elect Robert Williams, for a Better City." We concentrated on the East Side and the northwest quarter of the city, out to Dunbar.

Beyond the slate's literature, which mainly focused on mayoral candidate Tom Alsbury, we were able to prepare our own pamphlets. I decided to live dangerously and prepare two totally different pamphlets—one for the East Side and one for the West Side. The West Side pamphlets focused on the urban issues and putting a professional town planner on council, and carried the same slogan as the lawn signs: "For a Better City." In those days, the West Side vote was so hard for the NDP to get that we once had a lawn sign in Point Grey that read, "Your neighbour needn't know you voted New Democrat."

On the East Side, however, we were blatant. The slogan was "Vote for your side." Inside the pamphlet was a map of the city showing where the incumbent aldermen lived and an X showing that I was the only one living in the eastern half of the city. I have to admit that I lived in fear that the media would notice we were delivering a very different message in each half of the city.

The NPA was so entrenched that no one expected there would be an upset. The main City Hall reporter, Cliff MacKay of the *Vancouver Sun*, certainly didn't find my candidacy to be a threat, or of interest, but a young *Sun* reporter, John Taylor, did find me interesting and we later became friends. Taylor subsequently became an urban historian at Carleton University. Cliff MacKay would automatically support the establishment's new candidate for council—Vaughan Lyon, a former UBC Alma Mater Society president and a young executive with the *Sun* itself. There was also Tom Campbell, a wealthy real estate developer

Advertisement of candidates endorsed by the Vancouver and District Labour Council in the 1964 Vancouver municipal election. *Labour Statesman* (Vancouver), November 1964

who had run for mayor the previous time around. He'd made a lot of noise and had strong name recognition. And of course there was Harry

Rankin, the traditional candidate of the left, who was running for about the eighth time.

I sent out releases to the press regularly, and they started to get picked up. I recall one that I wrote up in an East Side laundromat arguing for aldermen who have ideals. My material started getting picked up by talk radio, including by radio powerhouses Pat Burns and Jack Webster. There was the string of nightly all-candidates meetings that were demanding, exhausting exercises, but wonderful training. By the end of the campaign I was reasonably skilled in both dealing with the issues and making an argument for myself.

The climax of those evening rounds occurred in an unlikely battle-ground in the heartland of the NPA: Kerrisdale. Kerrisdale was decidedly upper middle class and took their politics seriously. The biggest crowd of the campaign was at the Kerrisdale Arena. Lyon, Rankin and the others gave their traditional pitches. I decided to refine mine. I felt that I was on a roll, that I understood both the issues and myself, my own potential. I urged the crowd to think about the need for new people on council, a new generation with new skills like myself. More than that, however, I urged them to vote for someone who was not from their neighbourhood. For far too long, I argued, half the city of Vancouver was unrepresented: the East Side. From their response, I could tell that many of them would. It was on that night that Rankin and Lyon knew they were in trouble.

I had got a sense of a win two or three weeks earlier when I got a call from the city's main newsie, Jack Kanchikoff, who had the city's busiest news stand at Georgia and Granville. Kanchikoff asked for copies of my pamphlets to insert in every newspaper he sold. When your story gets through at that level, you know something is happening. And when "the crazies" start providing support, you also know something is happening. A big, blown-up photo of me had been posted on a downtown wall by a man who claimed to be a great phrenologist. He had thrown in his support because my head was shaped the right way. With Kerrisdale, the newsies and the crazies, it looked like a win was possible.

It was a fun campaign for us all. Here was a young thirty-one-year-old kid from the East Side trying to break the thirty-year West Side monopoly on City Hall. A relative handful of East Side friends and buddies were determined it could be done. Alan Cameron, a talkaholic retired miner, chaired the support group with loads of help from Lea Forsyth, her friend Mary Martin and all the regulars in the riding. Lea, who was the secretary of the riding association, considered it one of the best campaigns she had ever worked on. Fortunately for me, Lea's judgment wasn't always so sound, because a few years later she agreed to marry me (and for that I'm eternally grateful).

I also got help during that campaign from Alex Macdonald, one of the NDP's two MLAs for Vancouver East (who I would serve alongside later in the legislature and in cabinet). Macdonald was a lawyer who had been raised on the West Side and trained at Osgoode Hall, the son of a former Liberal attorney general and chief justice of BC. Macdonald's father put each of his three sons in a different party. Alex drew the short stick and ended up with us! We came from very different backgrounds. But in that first run for city council, Macdonald introduced me to his long-time friend Quon Wong. Quon owned Quon Wong Agencies on Easter Pender in Chinatown and lived on the Crescent in Shaughnessy. He delivered Chinatown for me because Macdonald asked him to.

It was a close race. Tom Campbell made it handily and I edged out Harry Rankin for the last seat on council. Vaughan Lyon, the new establishment candidate, tailed Rankin. The big news in the paper was that Tom Campbell had been elected to council. However, as Campbell said to me after an inaugural luncheon at Trader Vic's, "The big win was you, from out of nowhere." My friends and I celebrated on the East Side at our home base of the Rio Hall, and it was exhilarating for us all. At last, an East Side representative at City Hall!

At the same time, however, Harry Rankin and friends were furious. I had beaten Rankin by 1,300 votes. What I didn't know, however, was that the communists in town had held a meeting to determine if they would vote for me as well as Rankin. The decision apparently was to vote for us both. Had they not voted for me, Rankin would probably have won. (Indeed, there were that many communists in Vancouver in 1964.) As it turned out, I was no friend of theirs over the next two years, and they were furious over having lost out one more time. In the subsequent civic election, Rankin got elected and was an effective alderman for many years, though later on he was more the ornament and curmudgeon. The communists never forgave me, getting back at me when I stepped down from provincial politics decades later.

About two days before the civic election, Cliff MacKay and the *Vancouver Sun* establishment broke the big news story that I was a member of the NDP, which I certainly did not deny. The smart folks at the *Sun* editorial room clearly thought that this was sensational new information that would scupper the candidacy of this East Side whippersnapper. In truth, it was a benefit, for it brought out traditional NDP support to a greater degree than would otherwise have been the case. The editorial folks at the *Sun* would roll in their graves if they realized they were responsible for my breakthrough in politics.

Playing the aldermanic role was fun. It was serious. It was theatre. It was substance. I savoured all the parts. The best part of the experience was learning how to build coalitions with unlikely players. With the exception of Tom Campbell and myself, the council was with the NPA, the non-party party. The NPA group did not caucus, and soon it was possible to massage out a majority from us independents and some of their crew. The city's mayor in 1964 was Bill Rathie, a long-time NPA alderman with an accounting background. Having an NDPer on council was akin to heresy for Rathie. I looked forward to making his life uncomfortable.

One of the issues that bothered me greatly was the fact that one had to be a property owner in order to run for civic office. I had been able to achieve majority votes on council on a range of issues over my first year, which emboldened me to seek a change in the Vancouver Charter to open up the system. The Charter, a provincial statute, would almost automatically be amended by the provincial legislature in Victoria should I achieve a civic majority. There were some council members who were simply more egalitarian than others and some who were true-blue conservatives who had fundamental principles that guided them.

The egalitarians were Phil Lipp, an irreverent member of the NPA crew, and Tom Campbell, the independent. The "true-blue Tory" was Reg Atherton, a very principled man. The last person I had to quietly move to my side was Aeneas Bell-Irving. Over the years Bell-Irving and I grew to be good friends, which surprised many. He was a thoughtful, gentlemanly member of one of the grand old families in the city. He enjoyed reminiscing about the past and trading bold ideas about the future. I hadn't known that Bell-Irving, a pillar of the West Side establishment, grew up in the original family home on Alexander Street, which is now one of the grittiest East Side blocks in the city. In Bell-Irving's day, it was a fashionable address with a lovely view of the harbour and mountains close to downtown.

I worked on Aeneas Bell-Irving quietly for months, noting that it was unfair and improper in a democracy to not have universal citizenship for all people. Bell-Irving and his friends were in a stage of life in which they found it convenient to move from homes they owned out to apartments they rented. (In the 1960s there were no condominiums or strata-title apartments.) The argument that I put to Bell-Irving was that there was little doubt that his friends were good citizens; it was therefore entirely improper to disenfranchise them. That clinched it. Bell-Irving was on board.

When the time for debating the issue arrived, I was prepared and had all the necessary votes. The speech I gave quoted from the United Nations' Universal Declaration of Human Rights, thanks to the grand work of Eleanor Roosevelt and her colleagues. It was high-minded stuff that the mayor and his right-hand man, Alderman Earle Adams, weren't ready to stomach. The one thing they were sure of was that I did not have a majority. When voting time came, Adams was absolutely astounded that Bell-Irving, the critical vote, was supporting my motion. Adams was unable to conceal his contempt for my new friend, mumbling in a stage whisper, "Why, that dumb son of a bitch!" I was overjoyed, and considered it a huge victory, removing one more layer of second-class citizenship.

A far less important vote on council, but one I enjoyed immensely, happened much earlier: the expansion of the higher-density apartment zone in Kerrisdale. As a planner I wasn't convinced of the need and felt that the redevelopment that would occur would be better located elsewhere. The proponent of the Kerrisdale rezoning on council was Alderman Ernie Broome, a former Conservative MP. Broome was very sympathetic to the developer; blatantly so, I felt. Broome thought he had the votes, and I was afraid that he probably did. I realized that the one hope was probably an elderly loose cannon, Alderman Bert Emery.

Emery had been the founder of the Kitsilano Showboat, the neighbourhood amateur talent night that took place at Kitsilano Pool in the summer. He was known as Mr. Kitsilano, and cared about little else. In those days Kits was not known as the trendy neighbourhood that it is now, and was full of poor-quality rooming houses that begged redevelopment. I was convinced that Kits would be deprived of redevelopment if the Kerrisdale rezoning proceeded, and I knew that would be the one issue that would get Emery's attention. Truth be told, at that stage there was not a lot that could get Emery's attention because he was elderly and just drifted off much of the time.

I got up to respond to Ernie Broome's fulsome endorsement of the Kerrisdale project; he had spoken with as much passion as a lobbyist could procure. I made the point that there was no need for the project, that indeed Kitsilano was a better neighbourhood than Kerrisdale. Kitsilano needed new apartments near the beach. By the third mention of Kitsilano I knew I had old Emery's attention, so I repeated the argument: "If you vote for the Kerrisdale rezoning, you're voting against Kitsilano." Emery got it. When the vote came, again a critical vote made the difference. Broome just shook his head in disbelief.

Broome sent me a personal note right after the vote: *Meet me in my office after the council meeting is over.* I complied, not knowing what to expect, and Broome said, "Come on in you son of a bitch, and close the door." I did, expecting some kind of tirade. Alderman Broome opened his near-empty but rattling filing cabinet, pulling out a bottle of Scotch and two tarnished glasses. Pouring me a hefty drink, he slapped me on the shoulder and said, "That's the best piece of political work I've seen in ages. Once you got old Bert's attention with all that Kitsilano bull-shit, I knew you had the vote." While we were often on different sides of issues, Broome and I enjoyed each other's company immensely from that day on.

While in some ways I was the leader of the opposition on council, I mainly went after the mayor, who was such an easy right-wing foil. I also saw a major target in the then city manager, Gerald Sutton-Brown. He was the classic English bureaucrat, handsome in a young Rex Harri-son way, and with the same Savile Row tailor. Sutton-Brown ran a tight hierarchy of control. He had been director of planning from the days when only Englishmen needed apply for jobs in the planning depart-ment. So he had well-established background in extremely insensitive recommendations to council that ignored the community.

Even though I was now an alderman, I was still the kid who had worked at the service counter in the engineering department. From those earlier years I'd got to know most of the staff in the middle lev-els of the civic bureaucracy. There were all the branches of engineer-ing: streets, water, traffic, sewers, sidewalks, surveys. There was finance and assessment and taxation, which had always interested me too. My knowledge of the people and the hierarchy allowed me to become extremely well informed, saving me from many mistakes and providing me with solid information that most aldermen did not have access to.

Sutton-Brown, the planning department and engineers were onto a range of projects that I thought ill considered. Freeways were still on the civic agenda, and one proposal would have ripped through China-town, even impacting Robson Street, to connect to a new proposed First Narrows crossing of Burrard Inlet. That idea had to be consistently challenged, with the community finally winning in 1972. Urban renewal, the planning euphemism for bulldozing neighbourhoods, was in full bureaucratic flower in the 1960s. Another Englishman, Tony Geach, headed the city's urban renewal agency under Sutton-Brown. The planners and city manager were keen to bulldoze most of the Strathcona neighbourhood adjacent to Chinatown. Some massive public housing projects like Raymur public housing on Hastings Street had already replaced a chunk of the old neighbourhood.

I was convinced we needed no more of that tired approach which had already been discredited in the United States. They were actually blowing up massive public housing in the US while Raymur was under construction! I met and talked with some of the Strathcona residents who were being asked to sell out to the city so their modest homes could be torn down. Strathcona was the cheapest housing area in the city; one could own there without ever being able to buy anywhere else. The City was offering the people a no-win proposition: lose your house, get very little money, destroy your neighbourhood and replace it with massive ugly public housing.

As a planner I was furious that the City's bureaucrats were so far behind and were espousing policies that were already discredited in most of the Western world. So I took Sutton-Brown on with a vengeance, probing him in council over the lack of any social surveys in the impacted neighbourhood. The planners had simply carried out a "windshield survey," the planning equivalent of a drive-by shooting, and condemned the neighbourhood. Who were the people affected? What were their hopes and dreams? None of that was a concern. With details about the many affected people, I was able to question and challenge the city manager effectively. What social surveys were carried out? What are the detailed demographics? What about neighbourhood values? Why pour more traffic through an inner-city neighbourhood? And in the end, aren't we talking about class issues here, Mr. Manager? Aren't we applying different standards to these people simply because they are poor?

I was relentless on this issue; I had Sutton-Brown and I was damned if I was going to let him go. As far as I was concerned, he was a snotty Englishman that didn't give a damn about the people or the neighbourhood affected by his policies. I argued that it was the ultimate arrogance to simply drive through a neighbourhood and condemn it. It was crazy, I claimed, to take away the independence that home ownership gave people, regardless of how modest the housing was. At that time, Strathcona was unable to effectively articulate their view on the subject; I was able to be their voice at City Hall. On one occasion I dressed Sutton-Brown down with rigorous questions that he could not answer without showing how inadequate their planning and analysis had been. At the end of that session, his Savile Row suit was dripping with underarm perspiration. I knew then that I would win. As a result of these heavy sessions, Gerald Sutton-Brown indirectly acknowledged everything I said by establishing a new social planning department. Subsequently, the Strathcona urban renewal project was abandoned. It was a major victory.

The city engineers were also keen about getting voter approval of a new Georgia Viaduct about this time, an enthusiasm I did not share. The main reason for the viaduct was to overpass the CPR lines below. Those tracks and the Yaletown yards no longer exist, a prospect I encouraged. My primary concern at the time, however, was my firm expectation that the engineers would join the viaduct to the new freeway that was dumping traffic out on Cassiar Street farther east in the city. The engineers were considering connecting Venables/Prior Street and Adanac Street into what they called a one-way couplet. This was a device that had been very popular in moving traffic through inner-city neighbourhoods in Seattle. While it moved the traffic, it destroyed the neighbourhoods that the freeways sliced through.

To deal with that threat I sent personal letters with return envelopes to every household along both streets for the four-mile route. I got a huge response from the concerned citizens along the route and argued privately with the city engineer that I had to have a firm commitment that the couplet idea would not be pursued, otherwise I would fight against the referendum for the viaduct. The engineers agreed. That victory convinced me that one could often achieve more in the backroom than in the official forum, or council chambers. To this day, there has not been an attempt to cut a new traffic artery through the East Side. The city is much better for that.

After learning the lesson of the back room, I quickly put it to work on another important issue—the greening of the city. One summer day while on the Little Mountain viewpoint in Queen Elizabeth Park I was struck by the fact that the west half of the city from Ontario Street was all green while the huge swath east of Ontario Street was grey and barren by comparison. There were barely any boulevard trees on the East Side, which explained the difference. I was furious.

I talked to my old buddy Tom McDonald and said, "Jesus Christ! Look at this town! There's this class divide there, even the goddamned trees on the streets!" And he said, "You do know the reason the West Side is in such good shape, don't you?" I said no, not specifically. And he told me the story of how we were three municipalities historically: the City up to Sixteenth Avenue, Point Grey west of Ontario, and South Vancouver and Hastings Townsite to the east. And they were all administered differently. He told me about the work of Frank Buck, the first landscaper at UBC. Buck was an early socialist who was the first chair of the Point Grey Town Planning Commission. Buck had got Point Grey's tree-planting program underway earlier in the century. But the East Side was still without its trees and I was determined that would change.

By that time, I had a reputation as a scrapper and bureaucrats wanted to be on side if they could. The superintendent of parks, Stuart Lefeaux, was a bit of an autocrat, but I was determined to see policy changes that achieved my goals for my community. Nothing less than equal treatment with Point Grey would do. So I went down and saw Lefeaux at his house (a mansion) in Stanley Park on the Lost Lagoon terrace. I said, "Look, you know that I can cause you a lot of trouble. But if you develop a bureaucratic program for rolling out trees on the East Side of Vancouver, you've got my silence forever. I want to see those goddamned trees coming on the East Side." And then I said to him, "I'll tell you where I want the first trees planted. Charles Street, between Nanaimo and Renfrew." He said, "Why do you want that?" And I said, "Because it's a one-hundred-foot right of way, and there's a lot of space."

At first, Lefeaux tried to provide a rationale for the pattern that existed, arguing that the lack of curbs on the East Side was the reason for the difference. That was not entirely the case. Countless new curbed streets existed on the East Side, yet there were no trees. There were many streets that could readily be treed without curbs as well. Unwilling to face a big public fight over the shabby treatment of the East Side, Lefeaux privately conceded that there had indeed been a double standard. In exchange for avoiding an embarrassing public fight, Lefeaux was prepared to embark on a long-term policy change that would see massive planting on the East Side on a priority basis. And he rolled out dogwood trees on Charles Street. To this day, one of the joys of my life is to walk along Charles Street in East Vancouver and wrap myself in these wonderful fifty-year-old dogwoods. Now you go up Little Mountain and look out, and the whole city is green, even the industrial areas.

I was also able to push for more park sites on the East Side: additional land for Rupert Park, McSpadden Park and a recognition of the Still Creek ravine as a significant open space. The saving of the Langara Golf Course was also part of the agenda. A bigger fight I was engaged in involved False Creek between Main Street and Granville. I argued that it was a scandalous industrial slum in the heart of the city, insisting that it could become a new residential-recreational heartland. Rusting sawmills and beehive burners dominated the northern shoreline of the creek, while the surface of the waterway was totally covered with huge log booms, raw material for the nearby sawmills. The old Cambie Bridge, a low-level timber structure, traversed the middle of this industrial wasteland. I argued for a major clean-up, and that this was a terrible waste of extremely valuable land that could complement the changing downtown.

Those speeches got noticed by the *Toronto Star*, which had a weekend edition known as the *Star Weekly*. In one of those editions they focused on young politicians across the country who were making a difference. A young Robert Bourassa was on the page for Quebec, while a young Bob Williams was pictured opposite on the Cambie Bridge. The photo also showed the old Sweeney Cooperage, the last barrel maker in the province. One of the Sweeneys, who was a tourism spokesperson, responded that I was hopelessly irrational to attack these "job-creating industries." Fifty years later, most of the lands surrounding False Creek have been redeemed, creating one of the finest inner cities in the world.

The subsequent group from The Electors' Action Movement (TEAM), which took over council soon after I left, embarked on the rebuilding of the south side of the creek between Cambie and Granville. The change was transformational. The credit belongs to TEAM, headed by Mayor Art Phillips and supported by his able aldermen: Walter Hardwick, an urban geographer, and Geoff Massey, an award-winning architect. The TEAM council hired Doug Sutcliffe, the former CEO of Dominion Construction, to lead the entity that planned and rebuilt the south side of the creek. Their work and the creative work of MP Ron Basford and his appointees in turn transformed Granville Island. Those decisions were absolutely critical to creating the modern city we love.

The remaining challenge today is to envision the opportunity represented by the False Creek Flats between Main Street and Clark Drive. Re-establishing waterways in the flats, and seeing the flats as part of a larger, more diverse downtown could be as transformational as the TEAM work.

I found myself frustrated by some organizations in the city. The Pacific National Exhibition was one outfit that really grated, for they managed Hastings Park in a manner that often ignored the surrounding neighbourhood. Their board seemed dominated by the downtown elite gentlemen's clubs: the Terminal City Club and the Vancouver Club. More than that, the Hastings Racecourse also seemed a bastion of privilege. Jack Diamond's Jockey Club occupied a huge chunk of the park year round while paying only a modest lease rate and no property taxes whatsoever. To me it seemed a classic case of public lands being taken under unconscionable terms with little or no accountability. Conditions in the barns and stables in those days left much to be desired.

For an East Side resident, it was equally infuriating that one of Diamond's other businesses was his animal rendering plant farther west on the East Side waterfront. That particular plant spewed out a rancid smell that hung over much of the East Side on still summer days. Diamond, like many powerful people in the city, generally sent substantial gifts to council members at Christmas. These were gifts that I was determined to send back, causing the donors to claim that they simply didn't understand me.

Various types of favouritism caused me difficulty in those days. I recall that in my first winter as an alderman we had a particularly heavy snowfall, and right away there was a city snowplow on both streets by my venerable East Side home. Never before had I seen a snowplow in the neighbourhood. I called the city works yard asking for lower priority, more like I was used to. They were surprised; I was embarrassed, maybe unreasonably so. But it was the way I felt.

I recall the actual campaign for council when there was access to a wide range of groups, a time when partisanship was not so pervasive. The Rotary Clubs invited me to their meetings, and through those events, I was in turn invited to the Social Credit Women's Auxiliary meetings. The pay-off at the end of one meeting was when an elderly lady said, "Well, young fella, you've certainly got my vote, because you're a clean-living young man." I thanked the woman. "Do you want to know how I know you're such a clean-living young fella?" she inquired. "Well ... sure." I stammered. "Because you've got such good teeth!" Truth be known, I had had most of my teeth removed about six months earlier and had a sparkling set of false teeth. At subsequent NDP meetings, I would tell that story, concluding, "There, you see, those damned Socreds can't even distinguish something phony when it's staring them in the face."

One of the NDP meetings I attended around that time was chaired by Dorothy Gretchen Steeves, who, along with Grace MacInnis and Laura Jamieson, had been an MLA during the Second World War. Steeves, who at a later stage had been described by W.A.C. Bennett as the finest intellect he had come across in the provincial legislature, introduced me, a rookie alderman, as "that young dolphin moving deftly in a sea of sharks." High praise indeed from one of our finest legislators. I was having a lot of fun moving amongst the players in the city, beholden to none.

In some ways it was heady stuff. I was only months over the age of thirty-one, and I needed to talk out the escapades I was involved in. My regular friends and buddies were always there to keep me grounded. But the folks I counted on week after week to talk things over were my aunt Norma and uncle John Hayward, who never let me forget where I came from. Through their own character, they set a standard for me to relate to. Although I sought them out on a less regular basis, Jim Wilson and Alistair Crerar were always there as reference points, as well as Norman Pearson and the folks at the Lower Mainland Regional Planning Board. I also loved to drop in on the handful of planners in the Ministry of Municipal Affairs at a time when I didn't fully appreciate how politically vulnerable they were. Muriel Martinson, who was no NDPer, was one of the people I valued in that group. The head of the group, Don South, was a person I failed to fully appreciate at the time. South accomplished far more than I gave him credit for in those days. This was also a time when I was able to meet more and more of the eminent professionals: the architects in the city. I got to appreciate the work of Arthur Erickson and indeed was able to achieve rezoning for his and Lois Milsom's townhouse project on Point Grey Road.

It was a joyous time for me. I understood the players on council and got along with them well at a personal level. It was exciting to build coalitions to achieve significant goals. I reflect now on the kind of chutzpah that I showed all too often; it's a credit to the council that they tolerated and accommodated the brassy manner that I showed. In my second year on council, I hired a big bus to take council and the press on a tour of the East Side because I felt they really didn't know my half of the city. Most of them came along for the ride.

We visited the back lanes of Chinatown, the vulnerable parts of Strathcona, the foundry at Twentieth and Nanaimo that I subsequently got removed, and the Central Park interurban tramline that was still intact but had been abandoned (the line is now a SkyTrain route). My agenda for the city started becoming council's agenda for the city. These were exciting times, and more than that, I felt I was building a new base in the city for the NDP that was outside our traditional East Side ghetto.

I sensed new support in the West End, Kitsilano, parts of Point Grey and Dunbar. The political sands were shifting.

At the same time, it was fun to stick my finger in the eye of the establishment in creative ways. The mayor was a rather pompous, humourless man, so when I was acting mayor (Bill Rathie was away on a week's vacation), I declined the use of the mayor's limousine except to take a crowd of East Side kids on a Christmas Eve trip to Stanley Park and the aquarium, something readily noted by the *Sun*'s top columnist, Allan Fotheringham.

I was having the time of my life as an alderman but it was all about to change. Arthur Turner, the long-time MLA for Vancouver East, was determined to retire. And old Annie McGougan, Harry Whelan and the folks in the East Side were satisfied I should replace him. That meant that I was to run jointly with Alex Macdonald, the other MLA for the riding. Premier W.A.C. Bennett called the election for September of 1966. I proudly accepted the nomination for Vancouver East and there was no contest. I was chosen by acclamation at our traditional meeting place, Rio Hall. Little did I know I was about to face quite the culture shock in Victoria.

5. IN THE LEGISLATURE

The 1966 election was relatively uneventful at the provincial level, but for me in the riding it was the culmination of several years of campaign committees and working to elect others. There never seemed much doubt about the riding. Vancouver East voted NDP for both radical and conservative reasons. We were that village in the city who stuck with our friends, and these were our friends.

We had to find a campaign storefront and were lucky to find the old Spotless Cleaners branch empty on Hastings just east of Nanaimo Street. It was perfect, and of course we had Rio Hall in the south end of the riding. There were not a lot of troops working on the campaign, I recall, preparing the pamphlets and nailing up our campaign sign over the old Spotless material. Clint and Lil English were there on a regular basis, as were so many of our regular neighbourhood supporters. The canvassing seemed endless, but once we got into the swing of it, it was easy.

Alex Macdonald was a good campaigner. He had made a good impression as an MP in Ottawa. Similarly, he was effective in Victoria as part of a new breed in the NDP: a professional, a downtown Vancouver lawyer, a West Side resident whose father had been an attorney general earlier in the century. We both won handily, with Alex in the lead. And the NDP had not fared badly elsewhere in BC—our numbers were higher than almost any previous election, and we had sixteen seats.

The old-timers in caucus were supplemented with younger, more educated members who strengthened the opposition substantially. The old-timers in the opposition included Leo Nimsick from Kimberley in the East Kootenays, Randolph Harding from Kaslo–Slocan, Rae Eddie from New Westminster, John Squire from Alberni and Gordon Dowding from Burnaby–Edmonds. Alex Macdonald, Dave Barrett from

The British Columbia New Democratic Party legislative caucus, 1967. From left to right: Randolph Harding, Bob Strachan, Eileen Dailly, Bill Hartley, Leo Nimsick (bottom row); Frank Calder, Fred Vulliamy, Dave Stupich, Tom Berger, Ray Parkinson, Dave Barrett, Bob Williams, Ernest Hall, Alex MacDonald, Rae Eddie (top row). University of British Columbia Library, Rare Books and Special Collections, Dave Barrett Collection, BC 1964/24

Coquitlam, Dave Stupich from Nanaimo and Bill Hartley from Yale–Lillooet were relatively new. The new folks in the opposition ranks included Tom Berger and Ray Parkinson from Vancouver–Burrard, Eileen Dailly from North Burnaby and myself.

The leader of the opposition was Bob Strachan, the MLA from the Cowichan Valley. Strachan still spoke with a slight Scottish brogue, having landed in Nova Scotia as a farm labourer before moving to British Columbia, where he worked as a carpenter. I recall Strachan telling me about his time in Nova Scotia, which was close to being indentured labour. While Strachan did not have a university education, he was one of the most well-read people I had ever met, and I became very fond of him. Here was a self-made man, principled and committed to what we then called the democratic socialist movement. As an example, he was very keen about public auto insurance. He told me, "It's the reserves, it's controlling our own capital in the province. Insurance companies have to have huge reserves for long-term liabilities. So we can use those reserves, the capital, within British Columbia."

Victoria and its legislature were very different than Vancouver and its city council. First and foremost, it was partisan, partisan, partisan. Council is a round table where coalitions and consensus are seen as both possible and preferable. In the legislature it was winner take all, with party discipline demanded on both sides of the House. For me, moving from a coalition-building role in the City of Vancouver, all this was a big change. The old-timers were used to the kind of role they had, which was incredibly limited, in the W.A.C. Bennett–dominated legislature.

As a new boy used to at least having a private office and secretary at City Hall, I was offended to see how the opposition was treated in Bennett's hands. We had one room for fifteen MLAs to work in. We all shared a workspace around several large tables that were pushed together. A little bit of privacy was created by stacking up volumes of statutes between us. Bob Strachan had his own office and there was space for a few secretaries during session, led by Florence Riley, the only full-time person. John Wood, Bob's one researcher, had an office. But fifteen elected members sat around one large table and shared the telephones. Everyone just accepted this as their lot. Everyone except me, that is. I was damned if I was going to be treated that way. Once more, it was the second-class citizen problem. After all, countless bureaucrats had their own offices, and here we were, the elected representatives in a modern Western democracy, being stacked up like cordwood. I told the caucus that I was determined to do something about it.

Caucus members in those days referred to colleagues as comrades, the long-time designation in the CCF and other leftist movements. So it was, "Comrades, I'm not going to take this anymore." The reaction I got back from the old-timers was a slightly bored "It's always been this way, young man, and it's not going to change." I responded, saying that I was going to move out into the hallway. After all, the premier always walked down that hallway on his way to and from the legislative chamber. The next time he came down that hallway he was going to find a desk piled with books and papers, a long extension line and telephone, and myself dictating to a secretary.

Sure enough, that's what happened. Our working conditions became a major story; television cameras caught it all. Later that session, a wing of the building was being renovated and the carpeting was completed. I advised caucus that I was going to occupy the space: take it over and bring in a sleeping bag. Bob Strachan, who had been more than toler-ant of my bitching and complaining up to that point, argued against the occupation and the caucus shared his view. Nevertheless, by the next sitting of the legislature we all had new offices. For once, Bennett had lis-tened to the opposition. This new crew was going to make a difference.

While Premier Bennett generally ignored the official opposition, he seemed to be listening more to the new folks whose measure he wanted to take. I was still a rube, however, in my understanding of the kind of gladiators' forum our legislature actually was. My maiden speech in the House was very much the city planner speech. I recall speaking of cities as "the emblems of civilization" and was concerned that Bennett virtually ignored Vancouver and the metropolitan area. I argued for the involvement of the Province in building a greater urban region in the Lower Mainland.

Bennett usually sat with his back to the opposition when we were speaking, pretending to ignore us, but he did listen, because he later actually responded to my first speech in the House. I don't recall if he called me a city slicker in his response, but he certainly did in later speeches. His response was something like the following (we didn't have an official Hansard until we formed government in 1972): "That city slicker just doesn't understand that in some ways towns are just like pretty girls. There's only so many to go around. So when a young man can't find a pretty girl to wed, when there are no more verandas or girls, he just has to move on to the next town to find his opportunity." And that's the way it is in British Columbia, he said. In effect, Vancouver could look after itself, and the young bachelors would then move on to the less attractive ladies, the smaller towns of the province.

I wasn't impressed by the old man's response, thinking he just didn't get it. In more recent years, however, I've had to admit that maybe there was more to his argument than I'd given him credit for. It is clear that Bennett, when his back was turned to the opposition, was busy lecturing and providing sage political advice to his cabinet and the occasional supplicant from the back bench. Now and then the old man would get the urge to get serious and give a small lecture on a significant issue, such as debt. I recall him reflecting on debt for BC Hydro versus general indebtedness. Bennett argued that specific debt, debt that could pay for itself, as was the case with BC Hydro, was good debt, while general borrowing, which affected other spending on services, was bad debt. It was good advice. It stuck with me.

Most of the time, however, the old man would provide a simplistic political tirade, the same tirade, with modest variations, for the wind-up of any major debate, regardless of subject. The charge was, "You are socialists putting sand in the gears of progress. If you honestly put 'socialist' under your name on the ballot, none of you would get elected, none of you. I beat you in 1960, I beat you in 1963, I beat you in 1966..." etc. We called it the "flying fish" because the old man was in full flight, waving his hands wildly, as if throwing fish at the opposition. It was this capacity of the old man that often left our original members feeling beaten, with no fight left in them. For us new folks it was just more showbiz from Bennett—showbiz that was a little funny, and over time less and less effective. When the premier was in that mode, he never spoke in paragraphs, let alone sentences. He was barely rational.

I was still the city alderman in that first year, talking about issues, ready to follow up the discussion in the dining room or in the halls of the legislature. I soon realized that was not to be; it happened one day when I ran into the premier in the stairwell coming down from the upstairs dining room. I blocked the staircase and collegially started in on a follow-up discussion of one of the issues we had discussed in the House. The first emotion that flashed across Bennett's face was shock—shock that I should speak to him one on one. And then it was simply a closing down of all emotion. He just wanted to be free of me. At that point I saw the most soulless eyes I've ever seen in my life. I was shocked, stepped aside and let the old man continue down the stairs.

By the end of the first session I found that like most of my colleagues, I was exhausted. The premier was always determined to get the opposition out of the legislature by Easter weekend. To achieve that, he would call sittings day and night, often going around the clock. Our guys called it legislation by exhaustion. But the old man always got what he wanted: we were out of there by Easter. And Easter was payday. Our whole legislative allowance was paid out then and we were expected to be gone until the following January.

It was apparent that the premier was able to play the opposition like a fishing trip. He'd throw the bait, and we'd jump at it. I sensed it during the first session, but hadn't quite figured it out until the following year. What flooded over me was that my City Hall training was useless. The Bennett legislature was a battle scene, not a forum for dialogue. When it's war, you go for blood—that's what *this* legislature was all about. For me after that first session and well into the second session, it was pure culture shock. I had to rethink how I used myself in this new forum. I had to make a choice: take the bastards on, or be ignored.

But I wasn't the only new boy in the opposition. Much more notable was the arrival of Tom Berger, who now is rightly seen as one of Canada's great lawyers, jurists and royal commissioners. Berger arrived with the clear expectation of becoming the leader of the opposition. And some who arrived with him, like Ray Parkinson, clearly held the same view. Before long they had allies. Most notable was Randolph Harding from the Kootenays.

Bo Harding, as Randolph was known in the Kootenays, was an ornament for the legislature. He was one of the best orators in the House, had a lovely timbre to his voice and he had passion. That passion flared up when he talked about his sense of place and his roots. Nothing threatened Harding's sense of place more than the Columbia River Treaty, which flooded the Arrow Lakes and changed the West Kootenays forever. The lifestyle of the people Harding loved was never going to be the same again. No one in the House could equal the passion of the member from Kaslo–Slocan. But Randolph Harding had never fully accepted Bob Strachan as leader and seemed to have less and less time for him. Harding advised me that the leadership had been his for the asking, but he had turned it down. Whatever the case, Harding was probably convinced he would have been better than Strachan. For Tom Berger and Ray Parkinson, Harding's resentment was fertile ground to work. And work it they did.

Berger strengthened our ranks significantly, though not as much as he and his supporters thought. Berger was more the urbane intellectual with a strong academic background, very much the thoughtful lawyer. While there was passion there, it did not show itself readily, unlike the rural Bo Harding. However, W.A.C. Bennett knew that in the British Columbia of the day, Tom Berger did not represent a threat. The old man had Strachan's number, it was becoming clear, but he had Berger's number from day one, something Berger didn't understand. It was also becoming clear that the political world outside our caucus was taking notice of the challenge that Berger represented for Strachan's job. "Watch your back! Watch your back!" Bennett would yell at Strachan whenever Berger was speaking. The undermining of Bob Strachan's leadership was well underway.

Despite Bob Strachan's working-class background and his involvement at the grassroots level of trade unions, he did not share the support of the institutional hierarchy of the trade unions that Berger did. Berger was a lawyer and confidant for Pat O'Neal, the boss of the BC Federation of Labour. The Mounties had eavesdropped on some of O'Neal's activities, and O'Neal was concerned about that. Berger was privy to what that was all about. Regardless of the issue, it brought O'Neal close to Berger. O'Neal represented a potentially huge block of votes in any leadership challenge, a very significant base for Berger to build on.

On his own side of the House, the premier had a fairly impressive crew. Ray Williston was minister of lands, forests and water resources, a job that included the Forest Service, BC Hydro and the Columbia River Treaty. A former school inspector from Prince George, Williston was the workhorse of the cabinet. He had replaced Robert Sommers, the earlier forests minister, who had been jailed for bribery and corruption. Williston was very much a hands-on minister, one who both designed policy and administered the department. I concluded that we in the opposition had to show a similar capacity if the people of the province were ever to take us seriously as a future government. Subsequently, I spent part of a summer studying forest policy in Finland in order to show a comparable capacity, aided by a small grant from the Boag Foundation. In later years Williston would say that he and I were the last forests ministers in the province who actually ran the ministry.

Others in cabinet ranks were Minister of Highways Phil Gaglardi, Minister of Recreation and Conservation Ken Kiernan, Minister of Municipal Affairs Dan Campbell, Attorney General Robert Bonner, and Minister of Health and Provincial Secretary Wesley Black. The cabinet seemed impressive because this group and the premier were very able political players. But the truth is that in a democracy you have to build a cabinet with "the timber that the people provide you with," as Bob Strachan used to say. It was a very mixed group, their cabinet front bench.

Gaglardi was a high-flying, uncontrollable political force. A Pentecostal minister from Kamloops with a huge congregation, he seemed unbeatable. The premier, who was parsimonious on most expenditures, devoted all the Province's surplus revenue to highway and bridge projects. The province, barely out of the Depression and the Second World War, was hungry for the change that this aggressive works program represented. The challenging route through the Fraser Canyon was totally rebuilt, the Rogers Pass route through the Rockies was constructed, the Sea-to-Sky Highway to Whistler was built, the new Highway 401 through the Fraser Valley, the Port Mann Bridge, the Second

Narrows Bridge, the Deas Island Tunnel, Tsawwassen Causeway and Mission Bridge were all constructed during this era. It was an incredible legacy. Because the record was so impressive, Gaglardi felt no need to be accountable, treating the legislature with complete contempt.

When Flying Phil's department came before the House, he would turn his back to the opposition, place his feet on the marble wall and, with a toothpick in his mouth, comb his hair; in effect, democracy be damned. There was always doubt about bidding practices and favour-itism in awarding contracts for these huge public works projects, but Gaglardi would brush away the criticism like dandruff. Our old-timers in the House felt that Gaglardi was untouchable, a view that I did not share.

The bright new boy in Bennett's cabinet was Dan Campbell, a schoolteacher from Courtenay on Vancouver Island. Campbell's Comox constituency was a wobbly riding for the Socreds; it had been represented by the NDP on occasion. Indeed, rumour had it that Camp-bell had been in the CCF when he was younger. Be that as it may, Camp-bell was bright, aggressive and a quick study. Fellow planners and I had met with Campbell as he was thinking his way through bold legislation creating our present system of regional government. We all found him thoughtful and one of the more progressive people in his government. Nevertheless, as time went on, he became more and more aggressive with the opposition, a stance that I would not accept a year or two later when there were good issues and ammunition to shoot with.

At this early stage I was still constructive, and had a positive agenda I was ready to talk about with or without notice. As ideas kept popping out of me, Campbell took to labelling me the "young super-planner," dripping with sarcasm. I kept talking ideas and kept getting the sneering super-planner nickname. It took a few years before Campbell stopped using the label. Indeed, Campbell's fear was that he had actually given me a positive label that might be taken seriously by the public. Another prominent frontbencher was Wesley Black, the minister from Nelson in the West Kootenays. Black, with his booming voice, bulk and stature, was the quintessential old pol as he fingered his pencil-thin mustache in response to politically tainted questions, pronouncing, "You think I don't know the name of the game?"

For his relatively strong front bench, the premier had an unimpressive back bench. Minister of Public Works W.N. Chant had many of the symptoms of the aged, hearing nothing and understanding little. Herb Bruch from Esquimalt finally made it to deputy speaker but had an IQ that Dave Barrett would claim "only hit eighty on a hot day." Bruch would get so upset with the opposition in debate that he'd smash his drinking glass with his gavel. Other fundamentalists from the back bench would frequently slip into creationist mode.

For some of the new members in the opposition it made the legislature a contemptuous zoo. For others, it was truly representative of the wild diversity of Canada's westernmost province. At the very least, it meant that the NDP was more and more a force to be reckoned with. The new guys strengthened the opposition substantially, causing many in the media and the public to think the unthinkable: the NDP might be ready to govern. Indeed, at a later stage, that was the slogan Tom Berger used with the aid of his academic mentor Walter Young, an impressive political science professor from the University of Victoria. When the slogan was used, however, it had something of a boomerang effect. After all, no young city lawyer was going to decide that he was ready to govern—that was clearly up to the fairly cantankerous voters of British Columbia. "That's for damn sure," as Ma Murray, the editor of the *Bridge River–Lillooet News*, would say.

Berger was a determined young man, anxious to be in control. And he had many in the party anxious to see him take over. In caucus, Parkinson, Harding and others were keen supporters. Ernest Hall, the party's provincial bureaucrat, was equally keen. The party apparatus had frequently been the base to organize the malcontents and overly ambitious. That was certainly true in the 1960s. Bob Strachan had to face a caucus that now had shifting allegiances and a party bureaucracy that was not on his side. Despite my family history, I had doubts about Berger's heavy links with labour. I saw the needs of the province as far too diverse to be strongly beholden to one sector. At the same time,

I had no time for the excess privilege that capital often accepted or demanded. I also felt that it was too much, too soon for Berger to be seeking the leadership.

But pursue it he did, with Parkinson active in caucus and Hall active in the party apparatus. For Bob Strachan's people it was a shocker. Ron Riley, a long-time organizer, and his wife, Florence, couldn't believe the ambition of the new MLA and his colleagues. John Wood, for his part, felt that Berger hadn't even begun to understand the strange ways of both the legislature and the media that reported it. Berger, however, took the run at Strachan—too early, of course—and he failed. While he may not have met his own immediate goals, he left Strachan terribly damaged. Throughout that period. I encouraged Strachan to stay and fight, for I greatly admired this man who had lifted himself out of indentured labour.

Politics is often like the bullfight, however, and once damaged or weakened, a leader has little choice but to remove himself. Those of us who supported Strachan reluctantly concluded that was probably the case. Bob Strachan, on his own initiative, called a meeting of his key caucus supporters. The meeting took place at the home of Alex Macdonald, my Vancouver East colleague. Macdonald resided on the Point Grey Road waterfront, now an area full of multimillion-dollar homes. He was quick to explain to his socialist buddies that he bought the place after the war for only $10,000. Given the struggle of working people earlier in the century to create a political party of their own, it seemed the ultimate irony that the leadership of the province's socialist party would be determined at one of Vancouver's finest residential addresses.

The meeting included Alex Macdonald, Norman Levi, Dave Barrett, Dave Stupich, Bob Strachan and me, and together we concluded that Strachan should give up the leadership. Strachan would tell me later that it was my own view that led him to make that decision. By letting go, he effectively made the job available to Tom Berger. There was a leadership convention first, and I finally decided I would participate in it. Berger of course was the leading candidate, with a significant challenge from Dave Barrett, the social worker from Dewdney. A radical young student from Simon Fraser University named John Conway also jumped into the race.

I wrestled with the question of running for provincial NDP leader for a few months, finally concluding that if I could participate in the debate, I could present my own ideas to a larger audience. There was a chance of winning, but a slim chance. Of the incumbent MLAs, three supported my candidacy: Eileen Dailly from North Burnaby, Bill Hartley from Yale–Lillooet and Bill King from Revelstoke–Slocan.

Bill King had been elected in a by-election campaign that drew many of us over from the coast. I spent my time in Nakusp, an interesting little town on the Arrow Lakes where I'd worked as a summer student in the forest service. It was quite a scene, us city slickers helping out on the Nakusp main drag. A long-time socialist in a venerable clapboard residence at the entrance to the main street dubbed the local merchant street "Nickel Grabber Alley." Bill King, who was a railroad engineer, had a good base up in Revelstoke. The Arrow Lakes and Slocan Country were more of a challenge.

Bill Hartley and I forged a strong friendship working on that campaign. Bill Hartley had made a breakthrough by winning Yale–Lillooet. The dry-belt Interior had rarely voted for us, but Hartley built a solid base in his home riding, out from his hometown of Merritt. Hartley cultivated everything that moved or voted in his riding, finally capturing the support of the famous Ma Murray. Hartley talked Murray into coming up to Revelstoke to help out on the by-election. That was some achievement, for Murray's deceased husband had been a Liberal member of parliament. We wondered if Hartley and Murray would make it to Nakusp, for Hartley had perilously poor eyesight and Murray liked to regularly sip on a twenty-six-ounce bottle of Scotch. But they got there, much to the joy of us workers and the few big-city press folks who were covering the campaign.

It was great having the support of three colleagues: their ridings and Vancouver East gave me a reasonable initial base, as did my work experience in the Interior, which gave me a base in the Kootenays and a handful of other areas. There was no doubt, however, that I was starting from behind. Berger had a machine of sorts going for him that included Ernest Hall and the formidable Yvonne and Dennis Cocke from New Westminster. Nevertheless, we stitched together a basic campaign team with people like Ray Hellyer, a small businessman from North Vancouver who arrived out of the blue, keen about my candidacy. My cousin Janice Hayward jumped in, as well as Wayne Richards, who was producing an excellent neighbourhood weekly in Kitsilano, some of my planning friends, and mayors from the Interior of the province like Harry Lefevre of Rossland and Buddy DeVito of Trail.

Touring the province was worthwhile. It allowed us to develop a dialogue and define the differences between the major candidates. But more importantly it moved us all along the learning curve of understanding the enormous differences between the wildly different parts of BC, from North Vancouver Island to the Cariboo to the Kootenays. Any sense of "one size fits all" for this province soon disappears once you travel these regions. That's a lesson that Victoria bureaucrats and many newly elected politicians have yet to learn.

The NDP leadership convention was held at the Hotel Vancouver. It was pretty clear that Berger was leading the pack, with Barrett in second. I was third and Conway was fourth. I found that writing the leadership speech was tough. I wanted it to be philosophical and have some depth, not the usual tub-thumping rhetoric. That was probably a mistake, for conventions love the tub-thumping stuff. We were consistently different though. Our supporters wore cowhide strings around their neck with a Plexiglas photo of the candidate: *Your premier choice*. We turned out a newspaper every morning of the convention and slipped it under the hotel room door of every delegate before they got up in the morning.

On voting day, the newspaper headline read, "Strachan supports Williams." It was a neat twist. Bob Strachan was the outgoing leader and was neutral. But Strachan's wife, Anne, was definitely supporting me, hence the headline. As it turned out, by voting day Bob Strachan was supporting me as well. Once Strachan made his views known there was a bit of a groundswell. Cliff Scotton, a former assistant of Tommy

Douglas and long-time party operative, announced to the press, "It's a whole new ball game." But it wasn't.

Gretchen Steeves, a former MLA and formidable power in the party, nominated me. I was more than proud of that. At the same time, Steeves was little known by the younger generation, and meant less to the labour delegates who heavily favoured Berger. I felt ill at ease delivering the speech I did, and it left the crowd a little confused. Where was the tub-thumping rhetoric? While the pattern of results was as predicted on the first ballot, Berger was not as strong as expected, failing to win a majority. My key supporters were convinced that, though Barrett finished second, if he dropped out and supported me, we could have a good chance of winning by peeling away Berger's soft support. Alternatively, there was no way Berger supporters would shift to Barrett: they didn't consider him a serious candidate compared to their guy.

Be that as it may, I was more than satisfied that Barrett would never entertain the idea. I also knew our votes would not push Barrett into the winner's circle, but after the first ballot I supported Barrett anyway. I felt that Barrett had deeper roots in the party than Berger. Now, decades later, do I still feel that was the right choice? Probably not. Still, there was a visceral, emotional side to Barrett you could always count on, compared to the intellectual cool of Berger. That's probably what made the difference for me, along with our similar East Side roots. Sure enough, there were not enough votes for Barrett to win. Berger was the new leader, but for supporting Barrett, I earned the enmity of Berger's supporters for some time.

W.A.C. Bennett knew the province far better than Tom Berger, and he certainly knew the hinterland better. Berger's "Ready to Govern" routine was a little too arrogant for backcountry voters in the 1969 provincial general election. Walter Young and his young University of Victoria political science colleagues may well have been ready to govern, but the people of rural BC were not ready for them, and they were the ones who counted. Her Majesty's Loyal Opposition was reduced to twelve MLAs. It may have appeared that we were greatly weakened by losing the members we did. The truth is, we were not. More than that, it was a blessing that Berger was defeated in his own constituency, because it left the leadership question open.

It was a setback to be reduced to twelve members, including the loss of Bill King in Revelstoke–Slocan, but we prided ourselves as an effective "dirty dozen" who could play havoc with a leader and government who had simply been in power too long. We were quite a mix. Gordon Dowding was our "seagull" who could go after any garbage that was around. Not always the most accurate of legislators, Dowding spread his droppings wildly on some occasions. Nevertheless, he could filibuster more effectively than any of us, an ability often needed in legislative debate. Alex Macdonald was old family, erudite and had an excellent sense of humour. He was also a respected barrister, giving class to our group that we barely deserved. Leo Nimsick from the mining towns of the Kootenays brought with him a working-class rage about injustice in the workplace that harkened back to our radical beginning as a movement.

Bill Hartley was a kind of true-believer socialist who had been mentored by Gretchen Steeves and championed public auto insurance. Eileen Dailly, a schoolteacher from Denman Island who led the Burnaby School Board, represented the best of the teaching profession. (And the CCF had always been known for its many teachers and preachers.) Jimmy Lorimer, a lawyer and Burnaby alderman, provided a wonderful balance to us all because of his mellow humour and irreverence about the system. As he once said about his own profession, "It's all very nice to know the law, but it's far better to know the judge."

Bob Strachan carried the strength of his years in political wars and Dave Stupich provided an accountant's capacity into budget debates. Dennis Cocke, the new member from New Westminster, gave us a bit of business patina, for he came from a senior job in the insurance industry. Ernest Hall, our new MLA from Surrey and former party secretary, gave us a veneer of British Labour Party respectability along with his union linkages. Dave Barrett, my fellow Britannia High alumnus from the East Side, had joined the caucus a decade earlier after being fired from his job as a social worker at the Haney Correctional Institution. Barrett was acclaimed as party leader in the wake of the Berger debacle. We understood each other well, and we understood the job we had to do in both the legislature and around the province.

For my part, I was convinced we had to show the government had become corrupted by too many years in office, and that family, friends and insiders were getting rich from their connections and inside information. My work as a consulting planner in the Interior, which I did between legislative sessions, provided me with a great deal of information on what was happening in terms of real estate development in many Interior towns, especially those centres near Kamloops and Kelowna. I set out to show how the premier's children, Bill and Russell Bennett, became rich through favourable decisions by the Ministry of Highways and inside information about new highways and new intersections. The same kind of pattern was there with the activities of the sons of Minister Gaglardi.

No more philosophical speeches. This was outright war on the floor of the BC legislature and I had been taught by BC's most successful warrior-politician of the century: W.A.C. Bennett. Better still, we were the next generation. At first, I took on Bennett's scrappiest young minister, Dan Campbell, and it worked quite well. Often though, I would drop the small grenade on Campbell and then take off, looking after some planning consulting work in the Interior. As a result, Campbell would lament, "Williams is a hit-and-run artist." I was just balancing my two jobs (necessary in those days), but it proved beneficial, because I often wasn't around when he hit back. As a result, I was less damaged and ready for the next round dealing with the Bennett and Gaglardi boys.

There were a string of issues with Gaglardi, who would hypocritically hawk evangelicalism to a flock in the hinterland while looking out for himself and his family. His ranch on Cherry Creek was mixed up in using Ministry of Highways material on an illegal dam. The Gaglardi boys ended up owning land at numerous new highway intersections throughout the Interior—buying the land before the road got built. They parlayed these new sites into a string of motels, restaurants and gas stations scattered along the new routes. The Bennett boys similarly benefited from the enhanced values generated by the largesse of the Ministry of Highways. One parcel that Bill Bennett bought had no water frontage whatsoever, for there was a public highway running along Okanagan Lake in West Kelowna. But the Ministry of Highways let young Bill shift the road allowance back from the shoreline a couple hundred feet. All of a sudden, the road was sliced into tens of valuable shoreline lots. Until his final days, the younger Bennett lived comfortably on that former road right of way, Gellatly Road.

The many, many cases I placed before the legislature involved a lot of digging. It was absolutely critical that the data be impeccable. As a result, I achieved a great deal of credibility. Before long, the public was lining up to fill the galleries whenever I was tackling the government on these issues. An Australian songwriter who played the Arctic Club in Vancouver wrote a song about how the Bennett and Gagliardi boys enriched themselves along the provincial highways. When I started hearing that song on radio stations in the Interior, it was the equivalent of newsie Jack peddling my pamphlets at Granville and Georgia when I ran for city council. We would win.

It was a huge task documenting these numerous questionable real estate deals, but I was greatly aided by a fellow Henry George acolyte from the Shuswap, Mike Riley, who was able to gumshoe much of the material in the Kamloops region. In the Kelowna region, many of the senior staffers at Kelowna City Hall were anxious to help out. I worked as a planning consultant to the city when they had a superb mayor by the name of Dick Parkinson. The government of the day was not happy that I was able to play this double role of MLA for Vancouver East and professional planner for many regional towns in the Interior. Indeed, the mayor told me one day that Flying Phil Gaglardi had complained to him: "What are you doing hiring that red Bob Williams to do your planning?" It obviously didn't bother Parkinson. I continued advising them for some time. The planning work provided me with a substantial window into what was really going on in those various communities.

From my own work and the sources I had, it was possible to develop a catalogue of abuse and privilege attached to the aging Socred government. Not all that material got presented in the legislature. One example was the huge liquor distribution warehouse on East Broadway in Vancouver, which had earlier been the main distribution centre for Mc & Mc (McLennan, McFeely and Co.) one of our largest hardware wholesale companies. Mc & Mc financed or refinanced most of the Bennett hardware stores in the Interior. That refinancing allowed the younger Bennetts to expand their various real estate ventures that I had described in the House. In turn, the Mc & Mc company later sold off their major asset, the huge warehouse on East Broadway, to the government liquor monopoly. A profitable arrangement for them both. No reporters in the province unearthed this material.

The building of the case against the aging government and families of those in power was an intricate, demanding exercise that required hard work, accuracy and accurate sources. Any mistake could destroy an intricately built argument. On one occasion our seagull, Gordon Dowding, got into the exercise, claiming that the Bennett hardware company was supplying material to the Peace River Dam, then under construction. A judge was brought in to review the accusation. The judge admitted he had known the Bennett family personally for some time, but argued friendship would not bias any decision or recommendation. Then he concluded that Dowding's charges were unfounded, and went on to castigate me for other matters totally unrelated to the Peace River Dam. Gratuitous insults from judges and police are simply part of the history of the province, as we continue to see.

But W.A.C. Bennett was beginning to show his age. The sight of Bennett heading off to lunch at the Union Club wearing his traditional navy-blue suit and dark homburg hat with old cronies like Waldo Skillings seemed like a flashback to another era. Beyond that, the premier with his teetotal background wanted to end liquor and cigarette advertising, which made him seem a complete anomaly in the decade that followed the freewheeling 1960s. And with the material that myself and my colleagues were producing in the legislature, it was all starting to look like a very different place for the old man. It got to the point that when I got up to make a major speech in the House, Bennett would head for the door. I'd yell at him that he should stay, because I was going to talk about family and friends, but he'd swing his head quickly away and pick up speed in the revolving door on the government side of the House.

6. TAKING POWER

It was in this mood of changing times that the premier once more tested his government's popularity. In earlier years, W.A.C. Bennett felt he had the measure of his opponents. He was able to readily bait earlier leaders of the opposition and then nail them. With some of our members, he was able to play them like a symphony. Not so with the new group. He tried to pin the extreme socialist label on Dave Barrett, claiming he was part of the Waffle group, a more left-wing element in the party. Barrett responded by calling Bennett a pancake. Then Bennett called Barrett a Marxist, and Barrett asked, "Which one? Groucho, Harpo or Chico?" The old man wasn't able to play the same game, wasn't able to grab these newer players and put his label on them as he had in the past. The fact that Bennett was off his game also created unrest in his own ranks. Phil Gaglardi had his eye on the premier's job.

At long last, we in the NDP also started taking campaigning more seriously, searching out professional help. I chaired the media committee for the party and was overjoyed that we had Toronto advertising guru Manny Dunsky on board for our campaign, as well as an excellent pair of media people who had worked on campaigns for Ed Schreyer in Manitoba. Our radio campaign proved to be excellent. One of our radio ads began with the song, "Those Were the Days." Then the voice-over would announce that there had been good days under Social Credit, but times had changed, and they just weren't as good as they used to be. Print ads were very strong as well, centring on the theme, "Tell them enough is enough ... Vote NDP." All that, plus a happy warrior campaign from Dave Barrett, began to make the difference. Hans Brown ran our provincial office and did a superb job. Backup work in the office by Dennis McGann provided us with the range of talent we needed. There was almost daily communication between Dave Barrett and me throughout the campaign. He reported on the hinterland and his travels, I reported on the campaign in the big city. It looked better every day. The two of us thought we had a sure thing.

While our campaign began to lift, the Socred campaign began to slide. The old man became petulant and would not provide his itinerary in advance for the press. In about the third week of the campaign, the premier, in what seemed like a death wish at the time, was determined to take his campaign into Vancouver East, the NDP heartland. Speaking at Vancouver Technical Secondary School on East Broadway, after being jeered by the locals who were unimpressed by his limousine, the old man took on an even greater drubbing from the audience inside. Barrett's final stage of the campaign was at his home base in Port Coquitlam. To a huge turnout, the eloquent, passionate Barrett emulated Franklin D. Roosevelt with a plea that we had nothing to fear but fear itself.

We were all busy getting out to vote on election day. I was at Grandview High School of Commerce, and my wife Lea was at another local school. We got together, feeling sure that this was it, back at Rio Hall—a building bought with pennies in the Depression years by Annie McGougan and her socialist ladies' auxiliary of the CCF. How right it was to celebrate there. As our own numbers started coming in, we were more convinced than ever. Then radio and television results came pouring in from across the province. Big names were falling. Soon it was clear that even Phil Gaglardi was being buried by our candidate Gerry Anderson. It was a rout. While we had a huge crowd at the Rio Hall, a far bigger mob descended on Dave Barrett in Coquitlam. It was heady stuff for the dirty dozen and our new colleagues. After decades and decades of trying, the socialists were inside the gates. For us at Rio Hall, the work of stalwarts like Annie McGougan, Lil Winterford, Edna Nicols and the thousands of working-class heroes was finally paying off. We were all euphoric. The old Rio Hall had never seen such a celebration.

The next morning, I had a call from Dave Barrett. He wanted to get together for lunch and discuss the planning that had to get underway for the new government. That, I was keen to do. I sat down then and there in our kitchen at the back of our old house at 2158 Wall Street in the East Side, and on the back of a big, brown manila envelope, sketched out the nature of government structure and the cabinet line-up. In the background, on the radio, was the popular open-line show with Jack Webster. A woman caller, very distressed by the huge NDP victory, asked Webster in a plaintive voice, "Can they just have a meeting at the Vancouver Club and annul the election?" I roared with laughter when I heard it. But in a sense, it was an echo of what too many citizens had thought...Who did we think we were?

After Barrett found his way up our rickety back steps, he wanted the two of us to celebrate at the one spot his father had liked to celebrate at when he was a boy: the Only Seafood Cafe, deep on East Hastings near Carrall Street. The Only Seafood Cafe, with the neon seahorse above the door, is where the planning for the first socialist government in British Columbia took place. I'm very proud of that, as I'm sure Barrett was. I carried along my brown manila envelope with my planning and cabinet ideas. Unlike most administrations with thick secret files inside envelopes, this new administration had its plans on the outside! On later occasions, Barrett would often say to me, "You know, Williams, there's never been a government like us before in this country." I thought Barrett was exaggerating a little, as usual. But looking back, I think there was really something to what he said.

For those who remember the Only Seafood Cafe (which closed in 2009, following some irksome health inspection reports), it was little more than a soup kitchen in the heart of Vancouver's Skid Row. In 1972, the area was seedy and frequented by down-and-out alcoholics but was not the drug-infested disaster of today. For us, however, it was the historic heart of the city. As youths we would both come into town on the Burnaby Lake Interurban line that crossed through our Grandview neighbourhood, and we would both have slipped into the Beacon Theatre near the interurban terminus at Carrall and Hastings to catch the last of the vaudeville. I had joined the party only a few doors away from the Only, in what was then called the Holden Building and is now known as Tellier Tower. For Dave Barrett growing up, it had been a treat to leave his dad's market opposite the Powell Street Grounds and head out for lunch at the Only. In my own case, my birthday treat was to be taken two blocks east, opposite Woodward's, to eat at the White Lunch. Barrett and I had similar roots, and he graduated from Britannia Secondary two years earlier than I did, in what our yearbook editor Clive Cocking called "The Fabulous Fifties."

We parked on Powell Street and walked around the corner, up Carrall Street. It was just before noon and old boys that we used to call "rubby-dubs" were waking up in the various doorway alcoves. As we walked along, these wizened faces would break into great smiles, recognizing our Davie, the new premier. "Hey Dave, great stuff, good luck!" was the common greeting as these good old boys were coming to. As we walked by Pigeon Park, folks came up to shake Barrett's hand. It was a great lift for the two of us. And it was reassuring that the folks in Canada's poorest neighbourhood identified with us as their representatives. But the people also identified with Barrett's father Sam who had Sam's Market not that far away on Powell Street in Japantown. Sam was a wonderful character who frequently gave away fruit and vegetables from his shop opposite Oppenheimer Park. People who knew Sam knew that Dave had to be okay.

In the cafe, we headed for the back corner of the counter to order lunch. I pulled out the used manila envelope and went over the transition document. At each name and major point Barrett generally said, "Yep, yep, okay," now and then asked, "Why?" and then agreed. The transition committee took ten or fifteen minutes! Then it was on to odds and ends, details of the past few days, and the feeling that we were embarking on an adventure where there would be few differences between us two colleagues. Much later when I reflected on all this, I concluded it was much better to have the number-two role rather than number one.

The outline I put before Barrett concluded that we should have only our experienced MLAs in cabinet, which pretty much limited us to the dirty dozen. The dirty dozen became the first socialist cabinet in the history of British Columbia. Gordon Dowding made sense as our first speaker as he was a lawyer and fully understood the rules of the House. We also felt better with Dowding out of cabinet in view of earlier skirmishes where he confused the facts.

Dave Stupich made sense in agriculture because he was passionate about it, and actually had a degree in the subject. Eileen Dailly was a natural for the education portfolio with support from both trustees and teachers. Jimmy Lorimer, an effective Burnaby alderman, fit well in municipal affairs. Bill King was a superb, independent railway engineer from Revelstoke who, while sympathetic to labour, understood all too well the games they could play. Ernie Hall as provincial secretary seemed natural, while the thoughtful John Howard Society social worker Norman Levi was absolutely the right guy for the human resources ministry (Levi was not technically in the dirty dozen but had two years' experience as an MLA prior to the 1969 election).

Dennis Cocke had been our critic in health, and made a good impression on the doctors. Better still, Cocke had an excellent relationship with the management and leadership at the Royal Columbian Hospital in New Westminster. Richard "Dick" Foulkes, the left-leaning head of the Columbian, had been helpful on many health policy questions, providing Cocke with more depth in the sector. Former leader Bob Strachan got highways, which after the Socreds was seen as a major portfolio. It was broadened out to include all transportation issues and the huge issue of public auto insurance. Bill Hartley, who desperately wanted public auto insurance and had an insurance background, caught the lesser role of minister of public works. Barrett saw Hartley as too much of a true believer in no-fault public auto insurance. More than that, Barrett had a brother-in-law who was in the private-sector insurance business who did not hold the same views as Hartley. Leo Nimsick, who came from Cominco country in the East Kootenays, became our minister of mines.

I had been our resources critic for several years and wanted Ray Williston's portfolio. Williston had been the heavyweight in the Bennett cabinet; I was keen for the same job as minister of lands, forests and water resources. That suited Barrett fine. When I suggested that parks, recreation and conservation be included in my responsibilities pending our sizing up of the new MLAS, he agreed. I had concluded that our premier, like the one before him, should also be the minister of finance, otherwise there might be a fight about priorities between the premier and his minister. Barrett had some doubts at first, but then concluded I was probably right and that Stupich, the other logical candidate as a chartered accountant, would be better used in agriculture.

I thought that Dave Barrett was probably closer to the values I cared about, and the people and issues that mattered. I doubted Stupich would share these values. In a narrow sense, I thought Barrett as finance minister would make my life easier. The majority of the dirty dozen came to the same conclusion months later. The line-up on the back of the envelope became the first NDP cabinet in British Columbia with a nod of approval from the new premier in the heart of Skid Row at the Only Seafood Cafe (its neon seahorse sign is now in the Museum of Vancouver).

We had ten days or so before we were sworn in. For my part, I started making decisions right away. I needed an executive assistant, so I asked a long-time planning colleague and activist, Norman Pearson, if he was up for the job. Pearson had been with the LMRPB for several years and had recently completed the regional parks plan for the entire Lower Mainland (a plan that is now virtually in place). Crucially, Pearson was also a self-starter. I was overjoyed when he accepted.

I also needed an outstanding resource economist to start making sense of provincial resources policy. Mason Gaffney was a professor at the University of Wisconsin–Milwaukee when I first met him, but by 1972 he was at Resources for the Future (RFF) in Washington, DC. RFF was America's best think tank on resources policy and also had eminent New Dealers like Marion Clawson, one of the greatest thinkers involved on the Columbia Basin Project and the Grand Coulee Dam. Gaffney was an expert on resource taxation policy, and, like me, admired the early works of Henry George. I saw Gaffney as the best land and resources economist in North America. I told him we needed him in BC to carry out his research on the resource sector, to advise government and to impact the academy. I said we'd create an institute at the University of Victoria to get that work underway. Gaffney had already packed his books in a station wagon and was heading west.

I reached out to other colleagues in the planning field to help run the new government, including my long-time mentor Alistair Crerar. Crerar agreed to return to BC from the federal Department of Regional Economic Expansion (DREE) under the Honourable Allan J. MacEachen, a key member of the Pierre Trudeau cabinet. Jim Wilson, a former professor of mine and boss at the LMRPB who then taught planning at the University of Waterloo, also agreed to come back west and play a senior role at BC Hydro. And so it went—many young colleagues in planning were also asked to get ready to come home. People like Denis O'Gorman, who was then with Parks Canada, were needed for our new government. The list was lengthy. The interregnum between governments was not wasted. I was hiring and there was no one to stop me. That—our freedom to innovate—was the secret sauce that set us apart. No government since, nor any academic historian, has understood that.

During this interregnum, I became concerned about a large pulp company that was in trouble and looking for a buyout. It was the Columbia Cellulose Company, a subsidiary of the Celanese Corporation of America, which owned the Prince Rupert pulp mill, the Castlegar pulp mill and other assets. Pulp markets were in the basement, logging costs were high and the company was not making any money. The parent corporation in New York had wanted to get rid of Columbia Cellulose for the previous two years. I was interested in having the government take it over, leading me to call Ray Williston, the retiring minister of lands, forests and water resources, to urge him not to make any decision about the company during that period between governments. Williston told me flatly and simply that he was offended I would even think to ask him, because of course he would make no decisions in that interim period. I expressed my appreciation of his approach. He was a principled, hands-on minister, and probably the most competent member of his government.

One day I was passing by Blocks 42 and 52 in downtown Vancouver (what is now Robson Square). I called architect Arthur Erickson from a phone booth on the site. These blocks were owned by the provincial government and W.A.C. Bennett had declared they would house a fifty-two-storey provincial office building "just like the Bank of America building in downtown San Francisco." We city aldermen in Vancouver had not been impressed by that idea, so I told Erickson then and there, before I was officially minister of anything, that he was hired and that Ned Pratt, the designer of the fifty-two-storey building, would be fired. So much for process. But process never even crossed my mind. The fifty-two-storey building was a dumb idea and a shallow imitation of an American model. We could do better than that. Erickson fortunately took me on my word, began work and recruited one of his finest former students, Bing Thom, to come back from Singapore to run the project. Ten million dollars' worth of Ned Pratt's plans were junked. We embarked on the adventure to create Robson Square. I felt like Clark Kent in that phone booth! It was about then that I felt the only real limitation in British Columbia had been the lack of imagination.

Before cabinet was sworn in, I invited Bob Ahrens to our cottage at Langford Lake. Ahrens, who was head of the provincial parks branch, was a man I greatly admired who suffered the narrow-mindedness of both his cabinet bosses and the powerful BC Forest Service personnel, who saw our magnificent forested landscape mainly in terms of "fibre for industry," a dumbing down of the real value of our land. In earlier years, the Forest Service held full sway over the other ministries. Parks frequently lost to them in seemingly endless David-and-Goliath turf wars. Ahrens, who I visited regularly while in opposition, had a long list of proposed parks that had not got off the ground. At our meeting overlooking the lake, I advised Ahrens to go for broke, to prepare his complete wish list of potential new parks for the incoming government. Ahrens was amazed that after decades of barely being listened to, he would have all the sympathy and support he needed.

We talked about the Charlottes (now properly called Haida Gwaii)—Tlell River, Rose Spit, Naikoon. We talked about Cathedral

Lakes, Okanagan Mountain, the Coldstream Ranch and Cosens Bay in the Okanagan. We talked about Mount Assiniboine, Valhalla, the Monashee and Fry Creek. We talked about Cape Scott, Desolation Sound and Mount Edziza. We talked about Carp Lake, Kwadacha and the Spatsizi. At the end of the afternoon I told Ahrens we would go for it all. He could barely believe it after the dismal decades he'd suffered under the Socreds. But right then and there the die was cast. We would commit to double the amount of provincial parkland during our term of office.

In a sense we had to ask ourselves if we were going to be wreckers or builders. Were we going to undo much of the past, or were we going to build for the future? In my role I could spend a great deal of time pursuing questionable dealings, such as those documented in the courts between Minister Robert Sommers and BC Forest Products. Or I could pursue a more positive agenda. W.A.C. Bennett had often asked the rhetorical question, "Do you want the builders or the wrecking crew?" Dave Barrett and his team were clearly on the same wavelength as the old man. We wanted to be builders, but in our own way. And we were.

It was then time to be sworn in as a cabinet. I don't remember us having a caucus meeting during the interregnum. I don't think we did. We all gathered for our swearing-in ceremony, which did not take place at Government House but rather on the floor of the legislature. The new cabinet ministers, their spouses, a few assistants, the lieutenant-governor and the deputy provincial secretary, Lawrie Wallace, were there for the early evening ceremony.

The public was also invited to the legislature and we had what Barrett called a "bun fight," providing food and tea and coffee for the crowd of arrivals. The joy and excitement was everywhere. The folks who had fought against great odds for a socialist or social democratic world for British Columbia were out in force. You could barely move in the corridors of power. I was overjoyed to be greeted by one of the finest professors I'd had the honour to study under, Stuart Jamieson, a labour economist and urban sociology professor from UBC. Jamieson and his wife had made a special trip to Victoria in the hopes of seeing me, and excitedly grabbed me in the hallway. He said he and his mother had waited a lifetime for this, "and to have one of my best students in cabinet is almost too much for me to have wished for." High praise indeed. I also knew Jamieson's mother, Laura Jamieson, who'd been a wartime MLA for the CCF opposition and lived in my home riding near Victoria Drive.

Toward the end of the celebrations, Barrett and a few others agreed we had to see the old man's office, the space W.A.C. Bennett had occupied for many years. So we hiked down to the west wing. It was a terrible disappointment. The office had been scoured of almost any sense of its former life or personality. It was empty. All that was left other than minimal furnishings, strangely, was a small bellows, the triangular accordion for blowing air on the coals of a fireplace to get the flames going. "My God," I said, "it's just like the *Wizard of Oz!*" We all thought that the red-faced monster, breathing fire and flames in the legislature, was the real thing, but it had been blown up beyond all proportion.

Deputy Provincial Secretary Lawrie Wallace then handed out office keys to each new minister. I had taken the jobs of two ministers, Ray Williston and Ken Kiernan, and assumed I could take my pick of either the recreation and conservation office, with a stunning view overlooking Victoria's beautiful Inner Harbour and the Empress Hotel, or the lands, forests, and water resources office in the back of the building. Wallace chose for me, handing me the key to Williston's old office at the back. I looked coldly at him to clearly establish my position in future encounters as I accepted the key. "Lawrie, that will be the last decision you ever make for me." The deputy provincial secretary looked ashen and got the message loud and clear. I was no surrogate and not one to suffer the "Yes, Minister" syndrome that so many others did. The more attractive office with the beautiful view was going to Wallace's immediate boss, Provincial Secretary Ernest Hall. Wallace knew what he was doing, and turf can sometimes be everything in a hierarchy.

The next day Dave Barrett held a press conference to sketch out the cabinet line-up and the responsibilities of the various ministers. We had failed to allocate the key Crown corporations to ministers, so when

Barrett was called on that, he simply advised the press that he was taking on the job of BC Rail and that Williams had BC Hydro: "After all,
water resources is part of his portfolio." Barrett was quick on his feet,
and it often paid off. All that made for a substantial chunk of government in my hands, which suited me fine.

Although I had only been six years in opposition, it seemed like
forever, and my party had been waiting a half century for this kind of
chance. Whenever civil servants raised issues of process regarding the
roles Williston or Kiernan had, I made it clear: there was no more process. Now I had authority over every job that had ever been delegated to
them. That meant the remnants of the Columbia River Treaty, the allo-
cating of dollars for new parks out of the Greenbelt Fund, you name it.
It was now my process. On the Columbia River Treaty, I contacted legal
scholar Ian MacDougall, the grandson of General A.G.L. McNaugh-
ton, at Dalhousie University so he could spend his next break in BC
reviewing secret files at BC Hydro regarding the treaty. MacDougall's
grandfather of course had been the great critic in Canada about how
poor a deal the treaty was for us, and had prevented Bennett from making an even dumber deal at an earlier stage.

Then there was the family and social side of things—moving to
Victoria, kids changing schools, etc. Our daughter Suzanne had just
been born that year. We were still in our just-renovated house on Wall
Street—"renovated" when my Italian neighbours and I turned our
houses into duplexes during a City Hall staff strike. So, selling the Wall
Street house and buying a new one was actually a fun chore for me.
The Victoria market in real estate was very different than Vancouver,
partially because W.A.C. Bennett never increased demand very much
by keeping a limit on the civil service. While in opposition I'd bought a
three-room cottage right on Langford Lake for only $15,000, a bargain
even then. The Victoria market overall provided enormous opportunities. I convinced Lea to buy a mansion on Rockland Avenue, not that
far from Government House.

It was an early chateau gem designed by the same architect who
designed the legislative buildings, Francis Rattenbury. It was on three

quarters of an acre and had the remnants of a tennis court, five fire-places, a grand oaken entrance the size of a living room, a floor buzzer at foot level under the head of the dining table (so you could call the servant) and a separate staircase for "the help." It was stunning, and cost $65,000—about the price of a decent Vancouver bungalow at the time. I later found a blueprint of the original plan for the house, which included a "Chinaman's room" in the basement—that was the Victoria of that era.

With the baby, Lea found the house a terror to keep clean, and when answering the door, often got taken for the cleaning lady. As Suzanne got older, however, the sterility of the neighbourhood became apparent. She would look longingly out the window and only rarely get excited, when she would call out in delight, "Look, look, a kid!" But it became a place to celebrate events for the new government because of its size and grandeur. In addition, I bought a fine old player-piano. (Victoria is great for antiques—Barrett and I occasionally slipped out for evening antique auctions during early House sessions.) For our family, our first Christmas on Rockland Avenue was warm and memorable. Our mothers, my aunt and uncle Norma and John, my brother David and many others, including cousins, all came and stayed and joined in at the player-piano. We were celebrating a new era.

Our immediate neighbours were another story. Jack Mears, the owner of Oak Bay Realty, I believe, was on our left in another grand mansion, while on our right was Waldo Skillings and his family. Skillings had been a cabinet minister and confidant of W.A.C. Bennett in the previous Socred administration. Mears was neighbourly at first and invited us over for dinner at his home soon after we moved in. It turned out to be the only time we saw him—he had realized I was part of the "socialist hordes who had stormed the gates of power."

Good ol' Waldo was a special case. He refused to ever recognize us when we were out in the yard, showing the same kind of charm we had got used to in the legislature. Skillings's mean-spirited approach in the House caused Bob Strachan, then leader of the opposition, to label him Shovel Mouth, a term I thought appropriate. Skillings was a card-playing buddy of W.A.C. Bennett's, which seemed strange because the old man was a teetotaller and Skillings was a regular customer of the Union Club, the exclusive men's club in back of the Empress Hotel, where he was known for falling down the stairs. My analysis of this political friendship was that Bennett was a bit of an abstemious voyeur, and Skillings provided a window for the old man into lives far different from his. At any rate, Skillings was determined to be no neighbour of ours. What was kind of funny at the time was that Skillings had applied for unemployment insurance because he claimed he had lost his cabinet job "through no fault of my own." He was turned down, of course.

7. SUPER MINISTER

The back office over the rose garden proved in the end to be a far better location than the harbour-view suite—less crowded, quiet, easier to come and go, closer to the House and the restaurant. Lawrie Wallace had done me a favour. The office also had a big vault in the back corner which I used to yell into when I was hopelessly frustrated. When did that happen? Frankly, when I found senior bureaucrats not up to speed, people who shouldn't have been in a deputy minister's role. The Forest Service was particularly frustrating, and yelling into the vault after they left was cathartic. It didn't happen often, but it helped, I'm sorry to say. Later on, with Ted Young as chief forester and Peter Pearse as a consultant and royal commissioner, forestry became a pleasure.

The truth of the matter was we didn't have a lot of depth in the civil service when we became government. Many people who started out as mail clerks in a ministry became deputy ministers by the end of their careers. Initially I shook my head over the inadequacy of the public service. It was not long, however, before I realized what an advantage it was. There was nobody in our way, nobody to tell us that what we wanted to do was impossible. We could hire the best advisors in the world, along with the best consultants. And we did. These were incredibly exciting times working with the wonderful people we brought together. Furthermore, this was not Saskatchewan (forgive me); this was British Columbia, a far grander palette to work on.

. We knew where we were going. We were going to do what the party and our friends and people in our history wanted. We never thought twice about *not* doing anything. We had won where nobody else had, and we were going to deliver. The story is true that Dave Barrett got up on the cabinet table to dance in his stocking feet to celebrate our victory, kicking off the previous government's briefing papers, and asked, "Are we here for a good time or a long time?" It was a unanimous vote: it was to be a good time. None of us got ulcers doing what we thought was important.

Of those we brought in, Mason Gaffney needed the most care and attention. Gaffney was invited to become our in-house academic on issues of land and resource rents and revenues. Shortly after I had settled into my ministerial office, I received a call from a border official in a town that I wrote down as Crocus, Saskatchewan. The border guard said, "I have a man here from Washington, DC. He says he's coming to work with the minister of lands, forests and water resources in Victoria. Are you that person?" And I said, "Yes, I am." He said, "And you want him to come and help you?" And I said, "Yes, I do." So the guard yelled to the other border guard, "I guess it's okay, the minister wants him to come." A couple of days later, Gaffney arrived at our door in his station wagon loaded with books and moved in, before we settled him at our summer place at Langford Lake and then at the University of Victoria.

We set up his economic institute at UVic, where they reluctantly put him up in somewhat isolated quarters on their campus, and even held off giving him a library card. He was able to attract good people and give good advice, but had trouble meeting deadlines for a government that was moving fast, maybe too fast. So he basically stayed in the academic world, but effectively. The seminars Gaffney held were excellent and his advice to me when we got started was superb. I asked him, "Mason, what do I have to do to get ahead, to beat these bastards?" The professor's simple reply was, "Get up in the morning before they do." And that is exactly what I did. That advice served me well.

Norman Pearson played an essential role as my executive assistant (and later as deputy minister of lands). I couldn't have done it without him. Two additional executive assistants were added to my ministerial team: Bill Boutilier, a long-time friend from Vancouver East, and Wayne Richards, the editor of *Wednesday* magazine, a Kitsilano weekly. It would not have been possible to do my work without these people. They were talented, gifted, young, energetic and loyal. Working with this team was an endless feast—little wonder that I thought the only limit in British Columbia was our own imagination. Demanding as things are nowadays, I'm still inclined to think this, despite the narrow mean-spiritedness that prevails in Victoria today. My team preserved home base and extended our reach in the governmental system, and was exceedingly competent, a situation unfortunately not often the case with traditional political appointees.

At first, I kept the former minister's secretary, which was clearly a mistake. While the secretary was a hard-working soul, she truly loved (in a platonic sense) her former boss Ray Williston and found the transition difficult. Her conflicting loyalties made my job impossible. She also felt loyal to the boss of the giant mining and forestry company Noranda, Adam Zimmerman, who was as dangerous a beast as one could find in a corporate boardroom. But he was a charmer. Zimmerman would get front-line intelligence from the person guarding the minister's door. So the secretary had to be moved elsewhere in the system, to be replaced by my old friend May from Vancouver East.

With May at my office door I knew the regular folks from my riding would always be able to get in to see me. All too often I've seen successful politicians surround themselves with assistants who knew none of the people who had got them there in the first place. Did that mean May didn't get charmed by the likes of Mr. Zimmerman? No, but the East Siders always got the priority they deserved. Others who had difficulty accessing me said, "You've got a sentry, not a secretary." May prioritized access to me in the most unlikely ways. Old socialists had the ultimate priority—people like Nazar Patan of Rupert Street in my riding. Then other interesting folks such as Ray Jones, a former forestry executive who sent me a letter offering to help out our government. Any petty bureaucrat would've ignored it, but not May. The same system exposed us to the man who would design the SeaBus.

What about the more senior staff folks we inherited? There simply were not a lot of strong professionals at the helm of our public service in 1972. This tells us a great deal about Premier Bennett: much of the talent in his government resided in him alone. In my sprawling Ministry of

Lands, Forests and Water Resources, there was a mixed bag of talent. J.S. Stokes, the deputy minister in forests, had been used to having a minister who was a policy wonk, deputy, administrator *and* minister in Ray Williston, which left very little for Stokes to do other than be a conduit. Stokes's number two was more paper filer than a policy advisor. The secondary ranks had far more potential. It was not very long before those ranks were being groomed for the senior jobs. Another academic who I had gotten to know on forestry issues was Peter Pearse, an economist and forestry professor at UBC. Pearse proved to be an excellent support in tandem with the better people in the forests ministry.

The Forest Service, however, was a "service" like the armed services; it was a paramilitary agency highly geared to hierarchy. I had not appreciated what a paramilitary operation the BC Forest Service was until I attended their first large formal dinner at the University of Victoria. I was off in a corner in an intense conversation prior to the start of a buffet dinner. Staffers kept coming over to my corner, urging me to get my dinner. I was engrossed in the conversation and indicated I would eat a little later. What I did not realize, however, was the huge line-up leading from the buffet tables was growing and not moving at all because I, as minister, was seen as commander-in-chief and *no one* took a morsel of food until the commander had elbowed in at the head of the line. It was only at that moment that I realized what I had in the BC Forest Service.

The lands ministry I inherited was one of the Province's oldest ministries; after all, land was what brought the settlers here in the first place. The deputy in lands was a traditional civil servant of the day who had been in the ministry from his early days as a young clerk. It was a fairly hidebound shop where little change had occurred decade after decade. The old lands vaults and files were in the lower basement of the legislature buildings in Victoria. I had been unaware that there were *two* basements under the legislature. The first basement housed offices and the parliamentary dining room. The lower basement housed the lands vaults. I asked to see them.

The guardian of the vaults was grey-haired and elderly, and stooped when he walked. I met this chap at the cellar door. He was wearing gumboots. The ceiling of this lower basement was only five feet high at best, and the working conditions were abysmal. After my bent-over tour of parliament's sub-basement, I asked the guardian if he had ever complained about his working conditions, if he had ever filed a union grievance. "Oh no, Minister," was the reply, "because after all conditions are so much better than they used to be."

"How can that be?" I asked. "Well sir, the level you're at is below sea level, and I always needed these gumboots in the higher tides. But we don't have those problems anymore." This sounds unbelievably apocryphal. But in the fall of 1972, in our parliamentary sub-basement, that's the way it was. Those vaults were probably there from the time the building opened, so some public employee presided over that space, in gumboots, for most of the century!

There were some deputy ministers who were very capable and seriously adhered to the principle of providing their new minister with critical facts, knowledge, history and possible pitfalls. One such official was Valter Raudsepp, deputy minister of water resources, a rigorous, old-world engineer. At a later stage, water resources became the core of a future administration's first Ministry of Environment. I had not wanted it as a "line department" myself; I saw the overall priority for the environment to break through other line ministries in a more comprehensive and coordinated way. Raudsepp was a demanding, hard-nosed type, and he was an excellent deputy in that he readily knew what I would be interested in and always gave me the straight goods.

One of the early issues I faced in the water resources portfolio was a review of the Kootenay Canal project on the Kootenay River between Nelson and Castlegar. The Kootenay is one of the most productive power-generating rivers in North America because of the substantial fall of the river between the two towns. Much of the power of the river was harnessed early in the last century by the Consolidated Mining and Smelting Company (Cominco)—that had great power demands downstream on the Columbia River in Trail, where their smelter was located. As a result of the Columbia River Treaty, there was the opportunity to get even more power out of the immensely productive Kootenay River.

As a result, BC Hydro developed the Kootenay Canal project for surplus water to be channelled into a canal, and with considerable head, flow through new generators downstream. The entire capital cost of the project was being met by BC Hydro, but it had to share the benefits of the work with downstream dam owners.

When I came into office I wanted to see if there was any way out of this freeloading by Cominco. As a planning consultant in the region earlier, I uncovered "smoke easements" on the whole valley—private lands surrounding Trail. The company had established its right to pollute on the title of most lands in the valley. I found this was even more disturbing when, as a politician, I canvassed the riding during a by-election and frequently found terminally ill men answering the doors, men who were poisoned by the lead and other fumes from the mill. All this from the corporate owners of what was really stolen property.

Valter Raudsepp wanted me to know one critical fact: the licences for the immensely valuable dam sites on the Kootenay were originally allocated as leasehold sites with later reversion to the Crown, or the public, after a certain term—fifty years, I believe. The sites were worth a king's ransom: the Kootenay, in that short distance with the great elevation changes, had some of the most productive dam sites on the continent. Raudsepp showed me the old files, the early orders-in-council dictating the grants for the sites. Imagine, some thoughtful policymaker at the turn of the twentieth century—maybe one influenced by Henry George's arguments for public collection of the rent of land and resources—was protecting these huge future revenues for three generations hence! This public official, whose identity has seemingly been lost to history, saw to it that these locations were *not* to be given away in perpetuity. And Raudsepp still carried the history.

The tragedy, as Raudsepp advised me, was that those dam sites were reverted from leasehold tenure to full-title fee-simple land for the benefit of Cominco and its assignees, effectively forever. The rights (and revenues) of these dam sites were alienated, given away, as the government simply transferred the sites to Cominco with full, clear title, with no compensation to the government or the people of the province. It was grand theft. And like so many issues of corruption in British Columbia, it occurred prior to the fall of the Coalition government in 1952. As Tom McDonald had told me, he and other Tories and Liberals were offered spoils at the end of that regime. It was a time for paying off friends and distributing spoils and largesse, a grab of public assets. And one of the greatest energy-producing rivers on this continent was part of the spoils. To this day, Cominco and their assignees reap the benefits of that scandalous gift.

Another gem was shown to me by Raudsepp, a small statute called the Environment and Land Use Act, prepared earlier for the Bennett administration. One of my colleagues, a lawyer, called it, "the ultimate shit-hammer statute." And so it was—an incredibly powerful instrument that the Socreds had created. It was a one-page statute that gave cabinet extraordinary powers, allowing the government by order-in-council to decree other statutes null and void to the extent that they conflicted with new cabinet directives authorized by order-in-council. The statute essentially said that regardless of what any other provincial statutes said, anything undertaken under this statute trumps all others. I inquired of the deputy why on earth the Province would have a statute such as this.

His reply amazed me. Raudsepp said that Premier Bennett had been very keen to get a copper smelter in the province to add processing capacity, but copper smelters are the worst polluters in the world. He asked for a statute that would facilitate a smelter, without actually saying so, by preventing any environmental review. He wanted a green light from day one if we were going to develop such a smelter. And so, the Environment and Land Use Act came into being. Raudsepp further commented, "But Minister, statutes such as this can be used for good or for ill. That's your choice." And use it for good we did.

The Environment and Land Use Act was the vehicle we used to put in place a temporary land triage and systematically create what was labelled as the agricultural land freeze before drafting and legislating the BC Agricultural Land Reserve (ALR) that has preserved farmland in BC since that time. To poison or preserve, governing is all about choice.

The Environment and Land Use Act was also used to guide the conception of the Environment and Land Use Committee (ELUC) secretariat, the multidisciplinary professional group that became an exemplar in North America for approaches to integrated resource management. Guided by Raudsepp's preliminary advice, Norman Pearson looked at the legislation and realized that without changing a word of the statute, we could justify creating a staff under it to support actual integrated resource management. So we used the Socreds' own legislation to create this staff arm to do positive things instead of negative things. Pearson determined how to effectively coordinate all the individual ministries under one umbrella and then he did the personnel aspect of it, setting the whole thing in motion for a hiring spree to recruit the interdisciplinary people we needed. We said, "We're not hiring a bureaucracy; we're hiring a staff unit that will work together and apply the brainpower necessary to go after the issues."

Pearson and I agreed that our old planning colleague Alistair Crerar, who had agreed to join our new government, would head up the ELUC secretariat. Crerar became a "super deputy" in our government, coordinating the ELUC secretariat and the deputy ministers' committee. Crerar established a core team of seventy professionals who were unequalled at the time. It comprised a new Resource Planning Unit and a new Special Projects Unit coupled with a pre-existing Resource Inventory Unit, which conducted the Canada Land Inventory (CLI) assessments in BC (under a Canada-wide land inventory program that enabled ALR designation based largely on soil capability and sustainability for agriculture). Their project priorities came from the Environment and Land Use Committee of cabinet—through Crerar.

The ELUC secretariat became the management and staff arm of the Environment and Land Use Committee of cabinet, chaired by myself, and became a policy driver for the new government. Several years later, some members of that group became advisors on establishing the Commission on Resources and Environment (CORE), under Commissioner Stephen Owen and his deputy Denis O'Gorman in the Harcourt administration.

There was not a Ministry of Environment in our administration, but we saw environmental concerns as part of the entire resource management exercise—so we established the secretariat for the ELUC that comprised many disciplines including economics, planning, geography, forestry and biology. We created an integrated resource management and land use planning agency that played a high level "umbrella" role coordinating several ministries of government in developing responses to key land issues and needs. The agency, comprising about seventy people, was a new elite can-do group that was of a calibre and drive heretofore unseen in the Victoria bureaucracy. The nature of that work has been chronicled in a post-1975 BC *Studies* article written by Paul Tennant, a UBC political scientist. The article shows how the ELUC secretariat was formulated and how it worked. In essence, he concluded that we had developed the most sophisticated and productive management group in the new government.

With the Environment and Land Use Committee, I was basically running five or six ministries. And a lot of the ministers wanted me to run their ministries for them! Bill Hartley was minister of public works. He just said, "Do Robson Square for me, Bob." And then I also ended up doing the "Capital Precinct" in Victoria. There was no resentment around turf, and there was a need on the part of some of them for help. I worked very hard in other ministries such as municipal affairs on things like the Islands Trust, our Gulf Islands protective legislation, and I gave it its name to liken it to the National Trust in the UK.

The people who applied for jobs with the secretariat were the best and the brightest in Canada. We created the first great integrated resource management team in the country, if not the continent. Some people, like Denis O'Gorman, who we recruited from Parks Canada to work with Alistair Crerar in the number-two job in the secretariat, continued on as superb full-time civil servants, but were always considered suspect, as a product of our administration. O'Gorman would later lead the modern development of Whistler Blackcomb and the new townsite there as a world-class project. O'Gorman also led the pilot project to decentralize and integrate resource management through our experiment in the Slocan Valley (an idea whose time may yet come).

The truth is, I generally didn't hire "party hacks." Maybe one or two. Instead, I saw to it that we hired some of the best planners in the province. There was only a limited number of them in those days, so I sought out and hired professionals using regular civil service hiring procedures. Usually, including currently, it's a centralized hack-hiring game in the Office of the Premier. All governments do it, and you don't get the diversity, the energy and the innovation that empowers and supports ministers. Instead, we have a political spying system that empowers the centre.

The ELUC secretariat was a dynamo buzzing with energy to tackle challenges. When I think about it now, I may have been an arrogant son of a bitch myself, but I was doing work with some of the best people in the province. As much as I admired Valter Raudsepp for the critical background and due diligence he provided, our personalities were such that he concluded we would find it difficult working together over the long term. I am indebted to him for telling me the truth. In later years I have found too many careerists in the public service who would not be so willingly transparent about their feelings.

Raudsepp was square-jawed and concise through it all. He was a principled civil servant. He offered his resignation. Much as I admired him, I accepted it. No severance, no tears, just the conclusion of a job well done. This exceptional public servant knew how things should work in a parliamentary democracy. At a later time when I took my own leave from a deputy minister's role and as chair of the Insurance Corporation of British Columbia, there was to be no severance and no tears. A professional had taught me the way.

The first initiative we tackled using the extraordinary powers of the Environment and Land Use Act was the agricultural land freeze. I had faced the problem of urban sprawl into farmland during my earlier work as a planner in the Lower Mainland, first as a summer student with the LMRPB and then as the first director of planning in Delta. Recognizing the need to preserve agricultural land for the potential day California wasn't going to be able to produce enough food to supply BC, we had toyed with some controls on development at the LMRPB and in Delta. Once we were in government in 1972, we started asking, "What can we do province-wide to preserve agricultural land?"

The minister of agriculture in our administration, Dave Stupich, received a dusted-off report from his ministry urging the preservation of agricultural land throughout the province. The scheme had not been well thought out and was dated, but Minister Stupich ran with it publicly as a government policy commitment. He unilaterally announced at a press conference in Kelowna that his staff was preparing legislation. So, we had to hit the ground running. Inherent in his scheme was the idea that the farmers or landowners whose lands were designated required compensation. This became a major battle in cabinet between Stupich and me.

My team did the homework and showed that compensating for the Agricultural Land Reserve designation would "break the bank" and be far more than the Province could afford. Beyond that, the concept didn't recognize the principle that the Crown has the right to designate land use without compensation. And more than that, Stupich's implementation had been poorly thought out in other ways. Armed with the analysis from Norman Pearson, I was able to say to Stupich, "Your staff hasn't analyzed this properly. Development rights are owned by the Crown. Landowners don't have to be compensated at all because we can simply assert the right of the Crown in terms of development."

Stupich would then say, "Well, this is their retirement money, this is their pension, this is their crop insurance." I said, "Look, I can accept any of the above. If you want pensions for farmers, let's talk about it. If you want crop insurance, let's talk about it. But I am not going to talk to you about compensating farmers for foregone development rights when this isn't necessary." Barrett and the cabinet agreed that compensation was not on. As a result, the drafting of the necessary legislation to establish the ALR got shifted to my ministry.

We didn't trust the bureaucrats in the legal drafting branch at the time, so we brought in William T. "Bill" Lane, who was recognized as the best mind in municipal law in the province. He was solicitor for the

City of Richmond at the time and a former UBC planning professor. Lane came to the legislative buildings in Victoria and we went through fourteen drafts right there in my office. It received cabinet approval. The legislation directed the ELUC secretariat to handle the major process of soil and land capability assessment evaluation in conjunction with local governments. The overall ALR plan was completed during the term of government. The full working solution agreed upon by government would include a range of agricultural support programs (crop insurance, etc.) to aid farmers in other ways.

The full story of the formation of the Agricultural Land Commission was written up a few years later in BC *Studies* by a young Andrew Petter, a law student at UVic who had been a ministerial assistant in the Barrett government. The truth is, it was a chaotic and empirical process. Barrett wasn't one to cross *t*s or dot *i*s, and neither was Dave Stupich. In the end, our staff in the secretariat—Alistair Crerar and many other professionals—really became the technically able arm of the new government. The Environment and Land Use Committee of six or eight cabinet ministers, which I chaired and met every week, became a key force driving policy and implementation for the administration.

I was still a radical guy at this time, and wondered about putting in stronger rights for the Crown to take land for essential public purposes, such as land located within a greenbelt or an area identified for future highway purposes. One of my radical ideas was to use the land registry more effectively to allow government to become the replacement buyer to advance broader public objectives in these kinds of circumstances. So if a private parcel was going to be registered at the Land Title Office as a land transfer, government could step in and take the place of the buyer within two weeks at the originally agreed upon price. I had been doing that with the transfer of forest licences: when anybody sought to transfer a sawmill and the associated Crown lands and forest lands with it, the transfer deal had to be approved by the minister. I thought it was reasonable, as minister, that I could buy it at that deal price, and did so on several occasions. I sought to apply the same principle with agricultural lands, but the cabinet wouldn't buy that idea.

The biggest land acquisition we made at the time (which was the most substantial fee-simple acquisition in BC history, though it seems modest now) was the western part of the Coldstream Ranch in the Okanagan, which included Cosens Bay and those gorgeous twin bays on Kalamalka Lake. We were able to acquire it as a tremendous provincial asset now known as Kalamalka Lake Provincial Park. We also acquired the Minnekhada Farm on Pitt Lake, a large private hunting resort. We bought the heart of Victoria Harbour, Ship Point and the Reid Block, for public purposes. To their shame, Victoria City Council has done nothing with it in the fifty years since.

Following the land freeze and the passage of the ALR legislation, the Agricultural Land Commission came into being with Bill Lane as chair—reviewing the province's farmland base and applications to add or remove parcels. Abandoning the orthodox approach of only establishing an arm's-length board of directors, I established the role of a full-time executive director of the new Agricultural Land Commission for stronger provincial oversight. This position was filled by my long-time friend and colleague Mary Rawson, a planner who knew BC well and had a deep interest in food production. Rawson joined Bill Lane and three more commissioners. Like my colleague Jim Wilson on the BC Hydro board, these directly appointed directors played a profound role by making communications with the minister open and fluid. I had stumbled upon an important device for governance.

We devised a pattern in our government of creating executive directors for boards of directors in places like the Land Commission and BC Hydro—people who are full-time staffers in addition to having director powers. I have always liked hybrids as they allow power to flow and be applied in different ways. And that can be for good or ill, just as the Environment and Land Use Act could be. There were other matters, other boards, such as the BC Housing Corporation, that I played a role in. There we acquired an up-and-running land development and house building corporation, Dunhill Developments, and just built houses and apartments. It was very successful, made money and added to our low-income housing supply. It was not a bureaucratic solution.

It was a can-do, get-on-with-it approach, which was the way we did most things.

I probably inserted half the appointed senior civil service for our government. From the deputy minister of highways to the deputy minister of lands, half the deputies were people I knew from my prior professional work. We established a civil service that was all our own people. The weak civil service structure we inherited, the traditional process- and turf-oriented naysayer system was transformed.

We were government for only about thirty-eight months. They were the most exhilarating, exhausting years of my life. It has been said that I didn't suffer fools gladly, and I didn't. And I did not court with the captains of industry, which might have been smart, but was something I didn't have time for. I recall meeting with the CEO of MacMillan Bloedel—a former New Zealander, Denis Timmis, who had been appointed because he had worked with a Labour government in New Zealand. At the meeting he said to me, "But you're *our* minister—the minister for the industry—Mr. Minister." I made it clear I was not his minister, that my first obligations were to the people of East Vancouver who elected me, and next to the broad public interests of BC citizens who had a very different view of the world than Denis Timmis.

On another occasion, L.L.G. Bentley, who founded Canadian Forest Products, met with me and said he had had a tradition of meeting with Minister Williston every month "to discuss and determine public policy, and would you care to join me as my guest at my private hunting preserve in Austria?" I clearly indicated there would be no such meetings and no such trips in the future. As a result of sessions such as these, I was seen as an ideologue and no friend of business. What also scared them was that I was doing what they were doing—running forest enterprises as well as or better than they were.

After we were in government, I received a letter from Allan Blakeney, NDP premier of Saskatchewan, asking me to come to Saskatchewan and advise them on their public enterprises. Blakeney saw me as an expert in this field. I took Ray Jones, who was my expert, along with me and we analyzed the forest enterprises in Saskatchewan. As we did that analysis, we identified the terrible mistake the premier had made, even though he was one of our great politicians and administrators. The great mistake was letting the companies be run by civil servants, a role which requires an entirely different skill set than that of public administrators.

It was just another day in the marvellous Barrett government. There was an appointment in the Office of the Premier we were unaware of until we got a call from the premier's secretary Joyce Thomas a half hour before it was on. "Hi Bob, we have a meeting with the Baron, Lord Rothschild here in half an hour," Thomas announced. "Can you drop in for it?"

"Of course," I said, my own office being as close to Barrett's as anyone else's in the building. You'd almost think I was smart enough to have arranged it, but as far as I've already mentioned, I was clueless enough to have complained about it. At about 10:25 I slipped into Thomas's back office to see what this was all about. It seemed that the previous minister in my office had given the baron and his company, the giant corporation Rio Tinto, the authority to look into the power potential of two of our great rivers in the far northwest of BC—the Iskut River and the Stikine River.

I had helicoptered over both rivers the previous summer when I stationed myself in the northwest for a while. They were a glorious celebration of our wilderness and potential. We flew down the Grand Canyon of the Stikine, breaking out at the old acreage of Telegraph Creek where the river quickly braids itself into dozens of streams as it enters the Alaska Panhandle with glaciers breaking off all along its trough. It was, for me, one of the wonders of the world, and should never be dammed. Barrett and I had little time to talk before the meeting, but we implicitly trusted one another, so the lord and his corporate president were invited in. The guests presented us with two technical engineering reports, each about two inches thick, on the power potential of the Stikine and the Iskut. Their engineers had concluded there was great potential for power in both rivers, and their company was ready to pursue further studies about the feasibility of harnessing it.

Bob surveys the Stikine region at the back of the Alaska Panhandle near Mount Edziza on a helicopter stop, c. 1973. As minister of lands, forests and water resources, Bob played an integral role in the doubling of parks and protected areas in the province during the tenure of the Barrett NDP government. Bob Williams Collection

Bob surveys the Stikine region behind the Alaska Panhandle with Norman Pearson, c. 1973. Bob Williams Collection

I was able to advise everyone that I had had the opportunity of helicoptering over both rivers a year earlier and had some appreciation for their grandeur and potential. However, I had to advise them that BC was a public-power province and any development would therefore be with our own public power agency, BC Hydro. The baron lifted up the two heavy reports again, indicating that these bundles had been a huge investment on their part and they expected to get further endorsement to continue their work. I indicated I was unaware of any commitment from my predecessor Minister Williston to approve any further work on their part. I also felt the need to make it clear that this was a social democratic government, and we were committed to public power on our great rivers.

Our guests were dumbfounded and just sat there, not having anticipated such an unequivocal position on our part. They finally realized there was little to do but thank us and take their leave. The banker exited first—Barrett and I were at the side of the door. A fairly short man, Lord Rothschild turned, looked up at me and asked, "And what is your name?" The premier answered, "His name is Bob Williams, and he is my minister of land, forests and water resources." As the door closed on these important guests, Barrett was sliding down the door frame, holding on with one hand. Containing himself and hoping our guests were far away from the other side of the closed door, he turned and said, "Williams, do you realize that was the first time Lord Rothschild was ever told to piss up a rope?"

When I became minister, I was shocked we had no economists on the civil service payroll, only statisticians. I was also worried that once cabinet expanded from the dirty dozen and added an economic development ministry, the statisticians in the civil service would start pretending they were economists. Only Alistair Crerar, his staff and I shared sound economic training. So, what to do? Well, we strengthened our interdisciplinary group under Crerar, effectively put the most important areas of the province under him (and me) and limited the economic development ministry to the Northeast or Peace River and

Northern Rockies regions. As I said at the time, the area was not too important, and there were hardly any votes there for the NDP. Politically, it was more like Alberta than BC.

Our analysis of the Southeast was that it was the winner for productivity: it had rail now, was of good quality and extraction was not difficult—plus there were developed communities and infrastructure. The towns and the region in the Southeast hired the unassuming, immensely capable Harold Halvorson, the best analyst in the sector, to carry out a study for them comparing the coal mining opportunities in the Northeast and the Southeast. Halvorson made it clear that the Northeast was pure folly and could only harm the valuable Southeast, where the economic rent was the greatest and the public and private infrastructure was all in place. I made a point of meeting Halvorson and I found him delightful and with great capacity. But he was too modest and naive about politics, which in BC is a blood sport. We became good friends.

When the new ministry was created, its role was indeed limited to the Northeast of the province. Coal was the promising new opportunity in the Northeast, but access was costly and difficult. Gary Lauk, who was appointed our new minister of economic development, felt frustrated but accepted that the systems in place supported my views; otherwise we might have had a grand internal fight over Northeast Coal. The new ministry was left to work on the Peace River country and, we thought, the unimportant Northeast coal-mining area.

All this proved to be too smart by a half, for two major reasons. First, a group of Japanese companies wanted to create more competition in the sector as a means of driving down coal prices worldwide in order to benefit their steel industry. They encouraged new mining worldwide to service their ends, and not with really long-term contracts. Second, Don Phillips, the mouthy Socred MLA from the South Peace River district who we had labelled Leather Lungs for his long, empty orations about us socialists, became economic development minister when we were defeated.

As soon as he was appointed minister, Phillips asked what plans they had in the drawer. The only one, thanks to me, was Northeast Coal.

He was, of course, ecstatic that it was on his home turf: the Northeast could now be a big-time player. Thus, the biggest error in resource planning and public policy probably began under Bill Bennett and his inadequate Minister Phillips. Extensive private capital and public capital was misapplied on a grand scale for the Northeast Coal Development in the late 1970s and early 1980s. And while sometimes there may be a reason for a merger of public and private capital, that was clearly not the case with Northeast Coal, where both the public and private players were bamboozled at the ultimate expense to BC taxpayers.

Back in opposition during this time, I had several sessions with Halvorson and followed up on detailed questions about geology with respect to the project. Here were millions being spent by BC Rail on a new electrified railway through the mountains to link to CN and the coast. And huge amounts of private capital were being spent on the mine, Tumbler Ridge townsite and other infrastructure. Yet the fundamentals of the area's geology were hopelessly flawed. Halvorson explained to me that the coal was in a seam where they had not done enough drilling to realize there was a major fault. They'd plot the seam, and through sample drilling would realize the mine was wrongly located.

I roared with laughter and said, "You mean, the hole is in the wrong place?" Halvorson smiled and giggled a little and said, "Yes, I guess you could put it that way." I roared with laughter again. I smelled political gold and kept saying, "They put the hole in the wrong place." The government's iconic megaproject... And they put the hole in the wrong place! Some mine! Some government! How best to use this information? I knew the BC press wouldn't play it the way I wanted it played. My only hope was *The Globe and Mail* out of Toronto and their fine reporter Ian Mulgrew (later with the *Vancouver Sun*). I thoroughly went over the story with Mulgrew at the Railway Club in Vancouver. He thought it was a good one, but it would require engaging the minister, good ol' Leather Lungs. When Phillips's budget estimates came up for debate, I just kept hammering on him over Northeast Coal, saying, "The hole is in the wrong place," again and again and again. "The hole is in the wrong place..." Finally, in frustration, he blurted out, "I can't help it if the hole is in the wrong place!" That was it. Bingo! In politics, it was a classic gotcha.

The next day, the *Globe*'s Report on Business section—the premier source in Canada for this kind of story—ran the headline, "Northeast Coal in BC: The Hole Is in the Wrong Place." It was worth all the work. Phillips and Bill Bennett knew they'd been had. The following day, Victoria's *Colonist* featured on its editorial page a Bob Bierman cartoon of Phillips looking out, with a big hole in his forehead, saying, "I can't help it if the hole is in the wrong place." It was a classic win during those tough times of slogging in the opposition trenches. But the classic tale of Northeast Coal and the billions it cost has never been picked up by the press to assess in a substantive way. Consultant Harold Halvorson was prescient; he was correct, his analysis superb. It was the fast ferries fiasco times four, and way more dollars, as well as destructive toward the coal prices in the Southeast of the province.

The warning signs didn't stop the Province from proceeding and even involving the feds, including federal minister Ron Basford, in the project. I continued to watch Don Phillips carefully; he didn't seem entirely forthcoming and at the end of his time as minister I smelled a rat. Licences were being granted for timber rights in the Peace, and I was satisfied the process for doing so was not transparent. I continued intense questioning in the House about the deal, taking it as a far as I could given the information I had. Bill Bennett was very agitated by my questioning. I left giving the impression I'd be back with more information and questions that would prove him culpable, maybe even by the next question period. Bill Bennett had been a victim of my much earlier questions about his and his brother Russell's land dealings and favouritism in respect to grabbing public waterfront at Okanagan Lake. He knew that I got my facts right. Later that day, Don Phillips turned in his resignation as minister. Bennett clearly believed that I had more. And in our British Columbia press, no reporter connected the dots.

8. ACHIEVEMENTS: 1972–1975

We embarked on a number of projects during our brief thirty-eight months in power. I could write volumes, but instead I've attempted to distill some of the highlights into this chapter. My general tendency in government was to be entrepreneurial, and I built up a team of private-sector business consultants and lawyers we used for commercial acquisitions for the Crown. The first major opportunity involved the BC holdings of the Celanese Corporation of America, a New York company that had a wholly owned subsidiary in BC called Columbia Cellulose. Columbia Cellulose had two major operations in the province centred in Prince Rupert in the northwest and Castlegar in the southeast. Management of the company had been told by their board of directors to divest of the BC holdings, which included nine million acres of tree farm licence lands, a pulp mill in Prince Rupert, a pulp mill in Castlegar and fee-simple holdings. Also included were the logging operations and sawmills in each region, a head office and marketing capacity in Vancouver.

There was some private-sector interest in acquiring the Castlegar operation, but absolutely none in acquiring the Prince Rupert operation, which had historically always lost money. We took the stance that we would not approve a sale of only half the assets; that made us, the government, the only likely buyer. That prospect was acceptable to their management. We had consultants familiar with the local operation and had a far better picture of the company's prospects than the New York owners did. In particular, we had John de Wolf, a consulting economist advising the local regional district who we had quietly converted to our cause. John de Wolf had earlier been leader of the Conservative Party of BC and I had met him years earlier when we were both students at UBC.

We began negotiations and agreed broadly on the Crown acquiring all the assets for assuming the debt. The debt was in the form of debentures with Prudential Financial—some $65 million at 5.5 percent. That and a dollar would place all of these assets with the Crown. Our own analysis was that the log-market turnaround was less than a year away. I took a short ten-day vacation with my family and advised the comptroller general of the state of negotiations and asked him to simply handle it as a holding operation until I returned. No forests ministry staff had been involved in the venture—it had been me working with private-sector consultants, which is the reality of how we did things.

The bold acquisition proved too much for the comptroller general, who advised the Celanese Corporation, "There must be some mistake. The only group in the province competent enough to manage Colcel is MacMillan Bloedel, and there is no way the Province wants to proceed." When I returned, I found a very confused Celanese Corporation negotiating team, who were pleading to see the deal back on track. It was a blessing in disguise; I was able to get their European assets included in order to sweeten an already incredibly good deal. So we obtained all the BC assets, a recycling plant and a fine-paper and envelope plant in Brussels, plus a penthouse and a Jaguar over there (which we quickly sold off). All that for the dollar and the debt!

The lawyers working on the Colcel project advised me it was the most complex commercial deal in the history of the provincial government. It was a great success. By the end of our three-year term, profits were up to $150 million in total. It was a magnificent turnaround under public ownership. Ironically, people who'd already been in the secondary management level of the corporation were able to manage the turnaround. The talent was already there. During those years, there was in fact a capital strike in the forest sector, and most of the capital spending was undertaken by the new Crown sector that we had created. Between that and the intervention in woodchip pricing in the pulp sector, we maintained employment in the industry when no one else was doing so.

I enjoyed the discipline of these entrepreneurial exercises, and the government agreed it was worthwhile for the Crown to have a window inside the industry. So more acquisitions followed. We acquired the Crown Zellerbach assets in Ocean Falls, a company town on the Central Coast which included a dam and hydroelectric plant, a newsprint mill and the entire town. We developed a resource and regional plan for the area which would have linked Bella Bella, Shearwater, Roscoe Inlet, Ocean Falls and Bella Coola—a whole new transportation plan for the Central Coast—with local forest assets providing a wood supply. Unfortunately, we were defeated before the plan was implemented. I believe the bold initiative we planned would have had a profound impact on the Central Coast and Chilcotin regions. Only in the 1990s, when the NDP returned to power, did BC Ferries begin implementing a part of it.

We acquired Plateau Mills in Vanderhoof, one hundred kilometres west of Prince George. The Mennonite family who owned the mill wanted to sell. We replaced the potential American buyer with the same terms. Today, governments let the industry exploit, providing inadequate returns to the Crown. We built a new major state-of-the-art sawmill that was a huge success. The plant has been consistently profitable since that time. We acquired Kootenay Forest Products in Nelson, which included a sawmill and plywood plant, and forestry operations in the Kootenay Lake basin. We also placed workers on the board of directors of the company (a first in the province, I believe).

When we appointed two workers to the board of Kootenay Forest Products, we held a meeting with all the workers. I was standing on a stack of new plywood on the mill floor and then went out to the logging camp at Meadow Creek to find leaking buildings and slumlike conditions at their living quarters. Earlier that day, I had been in Nelson where executive offices were being unnecessarily renovated for the CEO. When I returned, I fired the CEO on the spot—workers could not be treated that way.

All of these entities were brought into a holding company under a manager I brought in from the E.B. Eddy Company of Hull, Quebec, who had formerly been with the H.R. MacMillan company and the earlier Powell River Company—W.C.R. "Ray" Jones. Ray Jones post-retirement was superior to the other folks in similar roles in the province. I was overjoyed to have him; he was simply a treasure for the new ambitious government. Jones had started his earlier senior employment with the Powell River Company's pulp mill operations and power plant up the coast. He led their team to do more value-added products in the industry when few others bothered. After the merger of the H.R. MacMillan and Power River companies, J.V. Clyne, a former BC Supreme Court justice became CEO of the huge merged company. Ray Jones as VP reported to Clyne, and wanted to explain what they had achieved in their new fine-paper plant on Annacis Island. To Jones's shock, Clyne was not the least bit interested and wanted to remain in the past with the land holdings and sawmills.

· That was it for Jones; he was offered a job in Hull, Quebec with the mill that the Westons owned, and moved east immediately. Weston valued him greatly and brought him to Britain for many years to carry out projects there. After retirement Jones lent himself out to international NGOs to help in developing countries. When Jones saw that I was building up Crown sectors in the forest industry, he pecked out a personal letter to offer his services. My secretary May showed me his ill-typed note immediately, and Ray Jones was hired right away.

These assets that were successfully managed in the public sector became part of a sell-off in the subsequent Bill Bennett administration, in the form of BC Resources Investment Corporation (BCRIC), which became Westar Mining and a monumental failure in private hands. What we had creatively acquired, successfully managed and made us $150 million while saving thousands of jobs, the new government then squandered away with poor management in BCRIC. BCRIC was given away to the public in a few shares each and was otherwise squandered into bankruptcy.

I was also interested in the forest industry itself and pulled together a couple of significant teams to examine that sector. One team was on forest policy and the other was in acquiring and managing forest corporations. Both were very successful. The policy side produced several task-force reports that were implemented, and the initiation and completion of a royal commission report (the Pearse Report) in 1976. Beyond significant rent collection improvements (stumpage and royalties) that followed from these reports, improvements in the tenure system also occurred. One interesting change that followed this work was the Timber Products Stabilization Act, which allowed the Crown to intervene in the pricing of woodchips (the residual wood from sawmilling that is the main feed or raw material for the pulp industry).

Our forest industry was historically a sawmilling industry. The pulp industry was not very significant initially, and the two sectors of sawmilling and pulp were not integrated. As the pulp industry grew, the two sectors became more integrated; however, a huge independent unintegrated sawmill sector was still in place in the 1970s. With a recession in lumber in 1974, it was likely that many of the independent sawmills might go under, partly because of the low prices paid for woodchips or residuals by the large pulp mills. The combination of poor lumber prices and controlled or oligopolistic pricing by the pulp mills made the entire independent sawmill sector extremely vulnerable. Our new statute allowed the Crown to intervene and establish minimum woodchip prices by region. During that recession, the independent sawmills went down like flies in Alberta and Ontario while surviving through the downturn in British Columbia. The pulp mills and the larger integrated companies were furious at the intervention, but the private sawmillers were elated. The pulp mills later punished the private sawmillers who spoke out publicly in favour of the legislation by not buying their chips.

I was also convinced we could do far more in the preservation of parks and wilderness, so we did. Total parkland in the province doubled during our time in office. We went from three million hectares to six million during our tenure, and then to twelve million under Mike Harcourt and Glen Clark in the 1990s, when I urged them to double it again. There had been no parks created for most of the twenty years before we took power in the 1970s. We brought in some new people to help Bob Ahrens and his team in the parks branch—people like Ric Careless, who had been a wonderful troublemaker in the Sierra Club, and whom Crerar and I admired.

One day someone in the head office shouted, "There's someone here who I'm directing to you." This fellow Daniel came in with these little specky glasses and a long trench coat, pure hippie written all over him. He had a huge bundle under his arm, and said, "Would you like to see some pictures?" I expected him to fling open his raincoat, but instead he laboriously undid the bundle and brought out absolutely stunning photographs of Cape Scott and Naikoon in Haida Gwaii. We hired him to take all kinds of photographs of our new parks. It was pre-election. We turned out picture posters of these new parks with the label, *This land is your land.*

That was the nature of the times: these people would show up out of nowhere, and we would be totally open to them. To me it was so wonderful. In a sense, what we were ready to be, when we were intrigued or excited, was opportunistic—which governments generally are unable to be. Civil servants are trained to be risk-averse, and civil servants are generally in control of the bureaucracy. My attitude with the bureaucracy was, "You'll find the money. I'm approving it." I just didn't care. They'd say, "Minister, it's not in the budget." And I'd say, "I don't give a damn."

Some of the parks established during those years were Naikoon Provincial Park in Haida Gwaii; the Spatsizi Wilderness Provincial Park in the Stikine behind the Alaska Panhandle; Kwadacha Wilderness Provincial Park in the Omineca; Carp Lake Provincial Park near Prince George; Cape Scott Provincial Park on the northern tip of Vancouver Island; Nitinat River Provincial Park on Vancouver Island; Mount Assiniboine Provincial Park in the Rockies; Desolation Sound Marine Provincial Park at the top of the Strait of Georgia north of Powell River; Top of the World Provincial Park in the Rockies; Okanagan Mountain Provincial Park; Kalamalka Lake Provincial Park in the Okanagan; Cathedral Provincial Park in the Similkameen, etc. At the more urban level, we dedicated 1,100 acres in the University Endowment

Lands at UBC for a park, now Pacific Spirit Regional Park, and acquired the Minnekhada Farm in Port Coquitlam on the Pitt River.

I was also responsible for pulling together a task force on the Whistler area, which at the time was a messy jumble of rough-edged subdivisions and the Whistler lift. The old lift at Whistler Creekside, as it's called now, was the centre of Whistler back then and it was a mess: inadequate utilities, sewer, water, planning, everything. Al Raine, the ski coach for Canada's Olympic team, wrote and asked us to save Blackcomb from logging. Yes, they were going to log all of Blackcomb! Raine and his wife, Nancy Greene, the Olympic champion from Rossland in the Southern Interior, came to me with a proposal for a new mountain development at Powder Mountain north of Whistler. I said it was premature; we had to clean up Whistler first. And that is precisely what we did.

Our ELUC secretariat team, led by Denis O'Gorman, worked on the question, and we brought in Sno-Engineering from Colorado to analyze the full ski potential of the region, including an analysis of the snow conditions. It became apparent that it had far more potential than we had realized ourselves. In addition, I hired Al Raine to become ski development coordinator for all of British Columbia. Raine proved to be the most capable brain for ski development in the province. He had toured all of Europe as a ski coach with the Olympics and with Greene, and remembered the exact orientation and the nature of most of the world's great ski resorts. He was very smart. A fundamental understanding of ski resorts went into the details of planning for Whistler through Raine's involvement.

Out of that, we developed the modern plan for Blackcomb and the Whistler Village, which was a former Crown-owned landfill area. That work showed we could link the new lifts with the new town centre and create a major resort. There were a lot of considerations, including community concept design and work to design roads, sewage and water supply systems. There was plenty of investor interest and O'Gorman had to manage an interim land freeze while the above was undertaken. To ensure orderly development of the new resort town, we froze the sale of

Crown land while the plans were finalized. O'Gorman joined in drafting legislation to create the Resort Municipality of Whistler, and Raine became a provincially appointed member of the new council, something never done before. Another hybrid! The current town centre is the culmination of that work, plus Blackcomb as a major ski facility. I doubt that any new ski facility or ski resort town in the world has been as successful as this one. It is consistently picked as number one in the industry. It alone represents 15 percent of our tourism GDP for British Columbia.

Also on the forest front, I was responsible for establishing the Burns Lake Native Development Corporation (BLNDC) in Burns Lake in northwest BC. There was no significant industry in Burns Lake in those days, but there were underutilized forests. We placed the timber in the subregion up for bid on a short-term basis, subject to building a major sawmill in the town. The best proposals came from Weldwood of Canada and another one from the First Nations and Métis in the region and led by a charismatic Indigenous leader, George Brown. The First Nations and Métis comprised 50 percent of the population of the area. We determined there should be a shotgun marriage of the two groups, and there was. The Indigenous Peoples, through BLNDC, became part owners of Babine Forest Products with Weldwood. We had to find people to train the local people in logging, milling and safety, and we did, ending up with the liveliest graduation ceremonies the town had ever seen. The mill has been a great success story, and all government loans to the Indigenous groups have been repaid. Tragically, however, the mill burned down a few years ago.

The six-foot-six George Brown was striking with his long dark hair and a stride that could cross a room in a single step. Brown had had a problematic youth and put in some time in jail. Once out of jail, Brown became a reformer aiding others who were in trouble, and undertaking work for the courts and justice system. His determination, aligned with a wonderful sense of humour, made Brown a real leader. We provided his band with funds for a business consultant and were very pleased with their business plan.

It was a time, once again, to be opportunistic. Better still, it was once again a time to use the talents of my deputy Alistair Crerar. Crerar was raised in Prince Rupert by his mother who ran a rooming house and his father who was a CN employee. When his parents drowned in a tragic fishing expedition when Crerar was about twelve years old, friends of the family determined it would be best if he remained in the rooming house. As a result, he was free to wander the town with young folks near his age, mostly from First Nations families. This background was invaluable in working with the Indigenous Peoples in Burns Lake—another opportunistic match that a bureaucratic hierarchy would never have made.

Some of these exercises led to the preparation of an economic development plan for Northwest BC—a region that encompassed the Celanese Corporation holdings in Prince Rupert, Terrace and Kitwanga, our new holdings in Vanderhoof with Plateau Mills, and the Burns Lake Native Development Corporation. Part of the plan for the Northwest included BC Rail. The former W.A.C. Bennett administration had begun a major BC Rail extension to Dease Lake, south of the Yukon. When I undertook a review of that prior plan, it became clear that the proposed railway extension was poorly located. The best forests were in the valley system to the west, and the best mineral prospects were in the valley system to the east. We concluded that the best answer was to bring in the federal government on the concept of building additional lines in the productive valley regions, and contribute our BC Rail line as BC's total contribution to the improved expanded national railway system. The result would have enhanced the assets of our new company Canadian Cellulose Co., which now had a supply deal established with the Celanese Corporation of America.

At no cost to British Columbia, we would have been nation-building from the Northwest: minerals would flow through Canada on Canadian rail through Prince Rupert rather than through the Alaska Panhandle, and BC's forest resources could be developed based on the benefit of lower-cost rail service in the Nass Valley. All this in turn might enable new hydro power development on the Iskut River in the region. The feds agreed to this new joint rail system, which would also enhance the northern port of Prince Rupert.

But not being aware of his father's earlier enormous error in building the earlier rail line in the wrong place, the subsequent Bill Bennett government merely saw this plan as the work of the NDP and cancelled this promising initiative to clean up the old man's mess with additional routes and federal funding. As a result, BC Rail had to subsequently write off the cost of the Dease Lake line. This was but Bill Bennett's first big mistake in BC's north. He went on to support Northeast Coal at Tumbler Ridge, losing hundreds of millions.

In the dying days of the W.A.C. Bennett government, the premier acquired the two city blocks that now house Robson Square. He directed the Ministry of Public Works to design a fifty-two-storey skyscraper, "Just like the Bank of America building in the San Francisco financial district." The ministry proceeded to hire prominent architect Ned Pratt to do so. As a former City of Vancouver alderman, I was not convinced of the desirability of that idea, so I replaced Pratt with Arthur Erickson, an architect of great talent who had not yet built a major building downtown. In my work in Finland, I had been impressed at how the Finns created significant projects for their people of genius, such as Alvar Aalto and his Finlandia Hall and Aalto University; and Eero Saarinen and the Helsinki Central Station. I had concluded that we should do the same in Vancouver with Erickson as the architect.

Minister of Public Works Bill Hartley turned over Robson Square to me from day one, because it was in the city. The present-day Robson Square is a result of Erickson's work and now is the true heart of Vancouver. When we subsequently celebrated the Whistler Olympics, Robson Square was the place to congregate. In Surrey they celebrated in our Central City project, their new city centre designed by Bing Thom. And of course Whistler had the village plaza championed by Al Raine and Nancy Greene.

The impact I had on BC Hydro was minimal in the 1970s. They were still in their US-Army-Corps-of-Engineers stage of wanting to build as many dams as possible. We did our bit. Seven Mile Dam on the Pend-d'Oreille River and the Revelstoke Dam on the Columbia River were undertaken during our time in office. The alarm bells were ringing, however, so we developed and implemented a rigorous process for forecasting demand for power. Recognizing the impacts of dams, we also mandated a major build-up in BC Hydro's environmental capacity that began improving decision-making in the organization. The new BC Hydro board reflected that by including people who were both skilled and had been shocked and concerned about the way BC Hydro had previously destroyed valleys and communities under the Columbia River Treaty power projects.

We also proceeded with the Kootenay Canal project, a power plant located between Castlegar and Nelson in the West Kootenays. More importantly, we appointed Jim Wilson, an experienced engineer and planner and a former professor of mine, as an executive director of BC Hydro primarily focused on the environment. Jack Steede remained on the BC Hydro board for this corporate memory. Two executive directors, another hybrid.

How did our government implement so many changes with such a slim provincial bureaucracy? We brought in our own people, that's how. Minister of Municipal Affairs Jim Lorimer brought in the immensely able Bob Prittie from Burnaby. Prittie was Burnaby mayor at the time and had previously served as an MP. Lorimer and I were very close, and we were also close to Prittie. As we often strolled about James Bay to take a breather from the House, Lorimer took my advice on most things. An example was the expansion of the boundaries of Kamloops and Kelowna. I was convinced that if these were going to be great regional cities, places like Rutland and North Kamloops and other municipalities around the main town had to go. I'd never thought that way about the Greater Vancouver region, where I see the need for diversity. But I'd given opposition speeches in the House on Dan Campbell's "Tinker

Toy" towns around Kamloops that he'd created for their Socred cronies. The amalgamations took place, but not without a political price. We would lose Kamloops and Kelowna in the next election.

It seemed simple: we stripped BC Hydro of transit and the bus system. Lorimer and I were both on the board of BC Hydro at the time, and transit was part of their monopoly. Under the management of BC Hydro (inherited from the BC Electric Company), transit services did not extend east of North Road at the east edge of Burnaby. There was no bus service through most of the Lower Mainland! The BC Hydro bureaucrats viewed this increasingly critical public service as a losing appendage to their core operations of energy generation and distribution. So we moved the transit assets outside of BC Hydro and into Lorimer's municipal affairs ministry. I remember sitting next to Lorimer in the House designing the whole fare structure for the greatly expanded Lower Mainland system.

Lorimer needed people to run the new system. We targeted Victor J. Parker from the old Lower Mainland Regional Planning Board to take charge of transit. Parker went about buying out bus companies here and there—the Vancouver–Victoria route, etc. Then we added Brian Sullivan from Alberta who was a rail and transit devotee and specialist (I later hired him when I was deputy minister for Crowns to initiate the West Coast Express commuter rail service to Mission). I also introduced Lorimer to Victoria naval architect Jim Hart, who was ready with the SeaBus design concept. All this in no time with able new people.

Lonsdale Quay was a project we created through the Ministry of Public Works to build the SeaBus terminal. Jim Hart had come into my office and my secretary May initially wouldn't let him in to see me. Hart had designed a SeaBus for somewhere else in the world and thought it was the answer in terms of providing good connection, instead of the bridge proposed for Burrard Inlet. We brought Hart in to work with Parker, who was running transit and the SeaBus project off the corner of his desk at municipal affairs. That's how we kept moving. Public works staff reported to me, "We're negotiating for the site for the ferry, and it also impacts Ocean Concrete and a whole other five hundred feet of waterfront." I said, "Buy it all! Buy it all!" We ended up owning all of that incredible waterfront and the opportunities that has enabled.

ICBC was subsequently headquartered in the back at Lonsdale Quay. But I wanted ICBC to be in Kamloops. We'd done studies about where the head office for ICBC should be. Crerar had done the bulk of the thinking, assisted by O'Gorman, and had concluded that it should be Kamloops due to its central location and good transport connections. So I said, "Let's spark the growth of Kamloops. Kamloops has always been deprived of being the real centre of the Interior by the Bennetts." We just about did it, but when I was away on vacation, Dennis Cocke got cabinet to agree to put it in his riding of New Westminster. After we were defeated, the bureaucrats in ICBC wanted to be on the North Shore because it was comfortable and a short walk from their homes. So ICBC ended up in North Vancouver, not New Westminster or Kamloops. That's the world of politics.

Lorne Nicolson was the minister of housing. The company he bought was Dunhill Developments and the owner was German-Canadian Vern Paulus, a very bright, very tough, demanding capitalist. But he was ready to sell. So we got, ready-made, the best and the brightest from that sector all at once—and no bureaucracy. We got their know-how in construction and their land inventory. I was one of the people on their board of directors, as was Mike Harcourt, a City of Vancouver alderman.

To manage the Dunhill holdings and expand the province's social housing supply, we created BC Housing and brought in a bright, young civil rights activist, Michael Audain, as assistant deputy minister of housing. When I had lunch with Audain, probably thirty years later, he talked about their first budget session with Barrett as minister of finance. Barrett asked Audain, "Well, how much do you need?" Barrett misheard him and gave Audain a multiple of what he asked for. When Audain found out, he said to himself, "My God, have I got a lot of work to do now." He never told Barrett that the premier had made a mistake.

Learn the business he did, after some years with Vern Paulus. No company has been more successful than Polygon Homes, largely due to Audain's involvement starting in 1980. From estate acquisitions and real estate holding to being the feistiest with the best of them in the suburbs with quite beautifully designed complexes, Audain reaped the value of the new densities. It was win-win. Audain and his wife, Yoshiko Karasawa, now fund an orphanage in Thailand that they visit regularly, and of course the Audain Foundation is a godsend in our arts community with their new galleries in both Whistler and North Vancouver.

With my socialist roots, I didn't realize I had entrepreneurial instincts until we were in government. The experience of taking over the big forest companies, going through sawmills with the big bosses and observing, "Well, if we tweaked this and if we tweaked that, that's more money on the bottom line." I learned on the job up at the top, the entrepreneurial side. And it became fun. One big, fun entrepreneurial project during those years was the *Princess Marguerite*.

The *Princess Marguerite* was the last steamship operating on this coast. It was the last of the CPR steamers and operated a summer service between Victoria and Seattle. It was a grand ship, the fastest of its size on the coast. But the CPR abandoned the service. So we thought buying the thing at the scrap sale would be a good way of keeping Victoria going in rough times, with all the people coming up from Seattle. The mayor of Victoria, Peter Pollen, also had an interest in buying the ship, we later found out. Once we started negotiating, we decided to try to pick up some of the land assets too: a large swath of land between what was the ticket office, the Steamship Terminal Building, all the way out to Laurel Point in Victoria Harbour. I negotiated the acquisition of the ship and land assets and pulled together a team to manage the new operation under BC Steamships.

In short order, we refitted the old ship in dry dock, painted the Union Jack on her stern (I thought the Americans would love it, and they did), put in fern bars and entertainment, gave free rides to local seniors, invaded Seattle with ancient cannons and the slogan, *The British are coming,* and had a successful service on our hands. I talked Washington Governor Dan Evans into coming up for the launch. I picked him up at the airport and we had a grand celebration with a whole gang of hacks and wonderful people on board. I remember Dan Evans saying, "What ministry are you in?" And I said, "Land, forests and water resources." And he said, "And this?" I said, "It is water resources, isn't it?" Our team leader on the project was the always amazing Norman Pearson, my old planning buddy.

It was a wonderful, fun project. The photographs of the time really capture the joy and the entrepreneurship of it. Subsequently, just at the end of our administration, I had lined up picking up the CN's last steamship on the coast, the *Prince George.* We were proceeding to decorate it like a Haida war canoe, full of Indigenous art for a new coastal tourist service. The inaugural trip was to be to the Queen Charlotte Islands (Haida Gwaii) to return their stolen totem poles that had been in Victoria. I did a press release in the middle of the election, saying, "That's

Bob at the inaugural sailing marking the renewal of service of the *Princess Marguerite,* a commercial vessel acquired by the BC NDP government in 1975 to maintain ferry service between Victoria and Seattle, Washington. Bob Williams Collection

Bob addresses the crowd at the launch of the provincial *Princess Marguerite* service, Victoria Harbour, 1975. Bob Williams Collection

Bob with Premier Dave Barrett at the launch of the provincial *Princess Marguerite* service, 1975. Bob Williams Collection

the next step." But the *Prince George* didn't happen. Bill Bennett came along and sold it as scrap to the pulp mill in Port Angeles that was on strike at the time. The mill used the ship for strike-breakers to reside on, inside the company wharves. How is that for creativity?

We were super entrepreneurial. Norman Pearson would pick up this stuff that I would spin off and run with it, and find the people to make it work. At one point, I was so aggressive with the roll we were on that I thought of taking our team to Britain and buying Rolls-Royce, just for the hell of it. We had so much cash in the till, and so much capacity on mergers and acquisitions, I thought, "Well why not?" It was up for grabs, and people didn't see it for the asset it was. So I phoned up Barrett at dinner one night, and said, "Dave, I'm really playing with the idea of making an offer for Rolls-Royce in Britain."

He said, "What?!" And I said, "Well, the team I've got is so damn good, and I'm satisfied that we've got know-how that's as good as anywhere in the world. It's terrific what we can do with a province like this and with assets like we have, and money in the bank." Then he said, "Don't you think you have enough on your plate already?" I said, "Well, no actually." And he said, "So, what's the justification? What's the linkage?" That's not the normal kind of question Barrett would give you. And I said, "Well, it's British, and this is British Columbia! Isn't that good enough?" His answer was, "Not quite, Bob. You've got enough on your plate." But that's the way I felt at the time. I'm more than satisfied that it was a great independent business consulting team we built for taking over and successfully operating the many forest companies we had acquired. It was a team that exceeded anything else in the private sector at the time... at least in these parts.

9. BYPASSING BUREAUCRACY

Our first government led by Dave Barrett got so much done in such a short time—truly, no others have compared:

- social housing on an unequalled scale;
- a giant of a new car insurance monopoly created almost overnight;
- the Agriculture Land Reserve, unequalled in North America;
- a public ambulance service and state-of-the-art ambulance vehicles (a model for the continent);
- the acquisition of pulp mills, sawmills, paper plants and a lean, able holding company for them all, all of them profitable;
- the unprecedented expansion of parks and wilderness, a doubling across the province;
- building the SeaBus;
- huge municipal amalgamations in the Kamloops and Kelowna urban regions to increase efficiencies;
- the establishment of BC's first major Indigenous-owned resource corporation, the BLNDC in Burns Lake, providing major employment opportunities for generations;
- the establishment of the Islands Trust in the Gulf Islands;
- the establishment of community resource boards at the neighbourhood level for social policy;
- the establishment of community health clinics as a new model in James Bay and Grand Forks;
- an experiment with the beginning of a model of local natural resource management in the Slocan Valley;
- an enormous expansion of transit out into the suburbs;
- the establishment of a new approach to labour: the Labour Relations Board;

- the establishment of various task forces and a royal commission on forestry;
- the establishment of the Foulkes Report on healthcare for the future;
- the end of corporal punishment in the schools; and
- the establishment of the ELUC secretariat, the best integrated resource management group in the country.

Writing these memoirs forced me to retrieve details from my mind that otherwise would be lost forever. And once put down on paper, it allowed me to theorize about issues like institutional bureaucracies, how they work, and their inherent power. And then it hit me: the reason we accomplished so much in three short years in the 1970s was because the bureaucrats were simply not there. The reason W.A.C. Bennett got so much done in the decades before was because he hardly hired any staff at all. And those who were there were limited in countless ways. The reality back then is that the bureaucracy was very thin. Bennett didn't believe in it.

To give you an example of how thin and how mean it was: shortly after we got in, I asked Bob Ahrens, the head of parks, to look at the winter Olympics proposals in Colorado. They had been turned down and we were being pushed for an Olympics at Whistler. So I asked Ahrens to report back. The report he gave me was just dismal, hardly any information. When I raised this with him, he said, "Well, we've not been allowed to phone long distance out of the province under W.A.C. Bennett." When I said, "What?!" he said, "Forgive me. I had to just go through newspaper clippings to advise you." It was that mean and that tough; civil servants couldn't phone outside of the province! Ahrens couldn't make even that kind of expenditure, and so was not empowered to make bold decisions, capable as he was.

The outsiders and consultants we hired during our brief thirty-eight months in power in the 1970s were used to getting things done, unlike the public service then or now. I have concluded that the bulk of the civil service is happiest just managing the status quo. After all, if you do something new, chances are you'll make a mistake. There will be no new mistakes if you do nothing. So the safest course for a bureaucrat is to do nothing, which is what much of the public service does. There are many obvious exceptions to this, as we all know, but the tragedy is still that we often lose the best and the brightest in the public sector, and all too often the system rewards the wrong people. The people who keep their heads down and do nothing tend to be the ones who make it to the top in the long run. But in the 1970s, the capability of the people in our bare-bones public service was substantial.

We established the country's biggest auto insurance company, ICBC. Who was the behind this initiative? Bob Strachan, a carpenter who came to Canada as an indentured labourer working on a Nova Scotia farm who made himself extremely well read. Strachan's executive assistant John Mika, a former reporter for the *Colonist*, at most had an English degree. Norman Botnik came from Saskatchewan Government Insurance. Many consultants too! And we pulled it off. Dennis Cocke as minister of health created the BC Ambulance Service, replacing the private sector. He had a team in Saanich developing the new design and infrastructure.

Norman Levi established neighbourhood resource boards—a new local model for social policy delivery across our urban areas—meaningful, profound, local democracy in the social policy jungle. He just did it with his people, new people. His executive assistant Joe Denofreo did much of the work. His other executive assistant, Ray Wargo, was a line worker who'd been moved upstairs and understood how inadequate the department was. Levi also had a terrific secretary with real executive capacity as well as the necessary sense of humour: the lovely Dorothy Sage who would go on to work for two lieutenant governors and in the premier's office for Bill Vander Zalm (a position from which she wisely took early retirement). The alcohol and drug group, under Norman Levi, was delivered by another new guy named Charles Barber, a future MLA.

There was no ministry for housing. We simply bought one of the best housing and construction outfits in the province, Dunhill

Developments, and were laughed at. But we had outside professionals who delivered. Michael Audain was one of them, now our great private homebuilder and a great philanthropist. My three new guys—Alistair Crerar, Norman Pearson and Denis O'Gorman—did all this work creating the superb ELUC secretariat. We developed the ALR through our shop, essentially the work of these three and of course our lawyer Bill Lane from Richmond. Isn't there a pattern here? We also placed the land inventory and soil survey unit with the secretariat. Those skilled professionals provided indispensable support to the ALR initiative based on their systematic soil and terrain mapping.

Compare this with the feds. During the Second World War, the feds rebuilt the country in no time. Canada became an industrial giant in the war effort, and it was done by bringing in private-sector executives— Dollar-a-Year men and women such as C.D. Howe. But there was also a special left-leaning service team designing for the post-war period. The government feared a continuing Depression in 1945. A team was created in 1939 for post-war recovery planning, and one of my professors, the social scientist Leonard Marsh, was on that team. What outcomes did this federal bureaucracy achieve? The Veterans' Land Act—the VLA—creating 1.6-acre parcels for homecoming veterans to build on and feed themselves. This was done here in Surrey, Burnaby, Richmond and Coquitlam. There was also university access for all veterans who wanted it—an enormous overnight growth of BC's tertiary education system. Mary Rawson and Alistair Crerar came out of this cohort, with thousands of others transforming themselves to join a formerly tight elite of professionals and academics.

Wartime housing was a rent-to-own program. Renfrew Heights and Fraserview are examples of whole neighbourhoods built under the feds. Programs for infill housing were established all over the East Side and throughout BC, called wartime housing at the time. It had never been done before, but we did it here in Canada in the days when bureaucrats delivered. By contrast, in more recent years the feds couldn't even competently create a gun registry!

An analysis of the above reconstruction is necessary for students of government to distill the lessons it offers. In our case in the 1970s, similar creativity took place at cabinet meetings where no bureaucrats attended. Later with subsequent governments, seeing cabinet attended by numerous bureaucrats was for me a reminder of why and how we got so much done. The public service in our government was almost irrelevant: we created the new policy instruments and brought in the new people committed to delivery. That's how it all got done. No bureaucrats were involved, and more importantly, none were in the way thanks to W.A.C. Bennett. No political scientist has figured this out—none.

One thoughtful academic who has a history of working in major corporations, Patricia Pitcher with HEC Montréal, considered the whole question of leadership in the private sector. Pitcher had been in a significant British corporation that had started in the Midlands, moved up to London and into Europe, and even crossed to America. That rise was fast under a very creative leader, who was replaced by someone more technocratic. Pitcher watched this same great company begin to decline.

Informed by this experience, when Pitcher looked at the Harvard Business School studies, she found herself asking, "Where's the beef?" What about all the petty jealousies and messy hierarchies she was familiar with? She entered a PhD program and wrote about her experience with different leaders in her former corporation. Her thesis was published as a short study called *Artists, Craftsmen and Technocrats*. She maintained that when it started out, her former company was led by an artist who saw patterns and opportunities that few others did. He had craftsmen who understood where he wanted to go and cleared the brush ahead for him. After he retired, a craftsman carried on satisfactorily. The craftsman became impressed with his technocrats and in turn left the leadership with them. Then the slippage began, and over time under technocratic leadership, the company completely failed.

Pitcher's thesis was you really do need artists to lead growing creative companies, aided by craftsmen who understand the vision of the artist. She had disdain for the technocrats, whom she saw as narrow and lacking. Worse than that, she concluded that technocrats tended to flatter and praise those above them, while doing just the opposite for those below them—a recipe for failure should a technocrat become the CEO. Pitcher admitted she had not a great deal of experience with government. However, from her observations she concluded it is the technocrats who typically get promoted within the civil service, not the artists. Canada's great public intellectual John Ralston Saul maintains that we have a pattern of leadership through what he called managerialism. Their speciality is simply managing—it's what they do. Our public service in British Columbia these days is loaded with technocrats that work within a managerial system, so don't expect reform or excitement.

Dear Jimmy Lorimer was one of the real pleasures to work with among a crew that got along so well. Lorimer was a Second World War veteran who was actually shot in action; a bullet grazed one of his nipples and shot half of it off. Barrett found out about it and called him old H.T. (half-tit) thereafter. It was that kind of place. Lorimer had the tendency to fall sound asleep in the legislature. I called him our bullshit meter. When the bullshit got too deep, Lorimer just fell asleep. The Burnaby–Willingdon NDP folks would sometimes visit Victoria to observe the action. All too often, their MLA would be sound asleep when the gang looked down from the galleries. Lormer's wife Cicely wouldn't miss a beat, cooing, "Ah…there's my tiger!" I felt very close to the Burnaby crew. After all, they were just across the street, with Lorimer living between Smith Avenue and Boundary Road.

We were *so* lucky to have the very capable Bill King as minister of labour. He saw through big labour in a nanosecond. I think there's an old thesis there—the craft unions versus the industrial unions. One of the first questions Dave Barrett asked King before he went into the cabinet was, "Where's your loyalty? Is it to the government or is it just to organized labour?" King made it very clear that he saw a deeper, broader obligation to the community and the government.

King took full control of the labour ministry. He set the bureaucrats up; this country boy from Revelstoke gave them lots of rope for the first several months, then fired most of them one by one based on solid grounds. Clean, quiet. It was a slaughter, but barely anyone knew. Publicly, they just resigned. The outcome was a whole new labour regime with a new deputy and brand new BC Labour Relations Board. Jim Matkin, an able academic who had carried out initial studies for King, became deputy labour minister. Paul Weiler became the head of the new Labour Relations Board. It was smooth as silk, this locomotive engineer running a new railway. He had stuff to teach us all.

I'm not so sure on health. We had a major study of the system performed by the sympathetic Richard Foulkes from the Royal Columbian Hospital. But I think it scared Dennis Cocke and he only bought into a small part of it. All this enraged Norman Levi, whose turf in some ways overlapped that of Cocke. He saw Cocke as terribly conservative. I interviewed Levi for two days many years ago and he was quite damning.

I had mixed views about my colleague in the two-member Vancouver East riding, Attorney General Alex Macdonald. When our government was defeated, I was publicly bitter about Macdonald for a range of reasons—some legitimate and some not. Now that I'm so far from it, it would be interesting to revisit those feelings, some of which were recorded in an interview I did with political science professor Jeremy Wilson. My views have changed; I've since developed a greater appreciation of what Macdonald did and how he benefited both us and the province. Macdonald saw through legal process in a common-sense way, which is immensely valuable for a government. While it's true cabinet (and Dave Barrett) were a little loosey-goosey in terms of process, there's little doubt we would not have achieved what we did had it been otherwise.

BC Petroleum was also an immense success and it was Macdonald who pulled it off. He hired some brilliant lawyers who really understood the nature of the task. It was essentially about nationalizing one inch of the pipeline—and that one inch changed the price. We were losing dramatically in terms of trade with the US because of a gap between the fuel price here in BC and the real price in the States. So the trick was to change the nature of the price. Macdonald and his colleagues created the BC Petroleum Corporation on the basis of an inch of the pipeline. Nothing short of brilliant. You don't have to take over anything other than an inch of the pipeline, right?

During that early period, we got a huge amount of revenue out of the BC Petroleum Corporation. And BC Hydro used to own the gas distribution system as well. (Later it was let go, like the railway, for a song. Most of these right-wingers cannot see past ideology to appreciate these instruments as the enormously useful development tools that they are.) BC Hydro is still barely used in the smartest, most creative way in that regard. Had we stayed longer in government, I have no doubt we would have become a substantial player in the gas fields in the Northeast. Rent collection from gas and petroleum would have been huge. It's still significant, of course, but what it might have been, we'll never know.

By creating ELUC, I had devised a cabinet committee that was in charge of land use, economic and environmental, and its integration. We couldn't have done the ALR without it. Crerar and his secretariat team of seventy to eighty interdisciplinary professionals in three units was unequalled in the country in those days. What we needed was a social and health policy equivalent, and that, we didn't have. Levi and I were leaders in our respective sectors. We had both concluded after our first two years in office that what we had to do was decentralize if we were to be relevant, meaningful and democratic—both in social policy and in natural resource policy. And we had hardly begun.

Eileen Dailly also brought in her own new people, including an imported American star if I remember correctly, as part of her education team. She made Pauline Jewett, a former MP, the president of SFU. Ernie Hall, of course, kept Lawrie Wallace as his deputy. Stupich kept Sig Peterson in agriculture, but my office severed him over the establishment of the ALR. It was probably halfway into our term that Barrett concluded he needed a deputy, so brought in Marc Eliesen, a prairie bureaucrat with an Ontario background. Eliesen knew he needed to be near the premier physically and he ended up in the basement below Barrett's office. I was still closer and could have my ten a.m. coffee sessions with the boss to get the royal blessings for all I was up to.

I'd conduct earlier sessions with Joyce Thomas, Barrett's long-time secretary. Thomas and I enjoyed each other a great deal, and Barrett and I went back too far, which made it problematic for Eliesen to properly do his job. I sensed the potential problem. As Mason Gaffney said, by getting up earlier and having access, I could then brief Eliesen later on the boss's decisions, new and old. Eliesen was part of Barrett's tribe, especially with their shared Jewish background, but this didn't trump my long, trusting relationship with Dave Barrett. I should have realized that this tension was a forewarning of what was to come.

One of our cabinet members who I liked and admired a lot was Norman Levi. A former tank commander, Levi went into social work after immigrating to Canada. He was seen as a strange bird who didn't worry about all the niceties of being a cabinet minister, because of the way he dressed—old trousers, sandals and long hair—and the way he talked. Levi was unfortunately not seen as the profound thinker he was on social policy. He had concluded we had to decentralize social policy so he created community resource boards. There are still remnants of it in Victoria, I think, in the James Bay area. It was a very creative approach to decentralizing delivery of social services.

Levi had come to the conclusion about community resource boards for social policy, and I had come to that conclusion about regional resource boards for economic and natural resource policy, initiating the Slocan Valley project toward the end of our time in office. Had we been re-elected as a government, there is no doubt in my mind we would have developed a decentralized provincial system for economic and resource policy, as well as for social policy. It's one of the great tragedies of our defeat that this never happened. Some of my thoughts about forest policy have been written in a 2018 report published by the Canadian Centre for Policy Alternatives on the failure in the industry and the need to decentralize to the regions.

Given how much we'd learned and how much we'd already done, one wonders what a two-term government might have achieved. And with the civil service, the base we'd established in terms of really governing and being creative and productive was sadly thrust aside by Bill Bennett. The intellectual leadership in the caucus around social policy, led by Norman Levi, had got to the point where we really wanted to decentralize and empower local people, just as I had realized in terms of economic and resource policy.

Reflecting back to our time in government in the 1970s, I can see that Barrett and Levi had great differences. Here they were, both Jewish, though Barrett was really secular whereas Levi was very much into the culture. The religion? Not sure. Barrett's religious education, it seemed to me, came from the Jesuits at Seattle University and Saint Louis University. And when he waxed politic in cabinet or caucus, it was largely about the Machiavellian side of the Jesuits (the only side Barrett saw of them, one sensed).

Both Barrett and Levi married able, strong women who could not be ignored. Shirley was the very perceptive, thoughtful woman behind Barrett, who he confided in completely and was very dependent on. They raised a close loving family of very good people. Levi's wife, Gloria, was very much the Jewish mother and power seeker who raised a wonderful loving family, too. And a New Yorker to boot! Of their children, David in particular was his mother's boy: had to seek and get power, had to know and use the right people. It was Gloria who urged me to support Levi for the Vancity board after I was elected, and I did. David was elected to the board, flattered the old-time board members and got himself elected chair. The role served him well and he proved to be good at it.

For Levi, it was more of a fight than it appeared to be to achieve what he wanted from Barrett. As with most of the players in cabinet, Barrett generally acceded to what we wanted over time. But Levi had real issues with Dennis Cocke, whom he deemed too conservative. The medical community required judicious management, and Cocke did provide that. Levi was able to get the community resource boards initiative out of Barrett without any cabinet process, but he always found himself running up against Cocke. When I think about it, it probably was running up against Cocke's bureaucrats more than anything that was at the root of their problems.

Levi was *not* a process guy, and understood the nature of institutional structure under Cocke far too clearly. When I hung around the John Howard Society with Levi, I got the picture of too many young men trapped by process and systems they could not free themselves from. Levi understood the inadequacies of all that and the guys he helped would do anything for him, like working in political campaigns. (There were always a few rough-hewn guys working their butts off for him.) Much later, Levi was one of the drivers of the "unplug the Cocke machine" gang, getting rid of Yvonne Cocke as provincial NDP president. I think his involvement both surprised and hurt Dennis and Yvonne.

Were Levi and Barrett close? I don't really think so. A few years later, visiting Levi at his B & B home in Victoria, it was clear that there was very little social contact between him and Barrett. While they lived in the same small town a few miles from one another, they never socialized. Revisiting all this now, I find it apparent that they had different views of the world, including the nature and understanding of institutions and bureaucratic structures. I knew whose side I was on in those kinds of differences. The Cockes were close to big labour, unlike Levi. Cocke was also close to NDP backbench MLA Rosemary Brown. They shared a duplex in Victoria for some time, so he was also Brown's voice in cabinet. Did I sometimes yell, "Author, author," after some of Cocke's speeches in cabinet? I think so. It was more frequently Brown's voice we heard, but sometimes Yvonne Cocke's as well.

And if he would readily parrot them, perhaps he also parroted his officials when dealing with Levi. I think so. I recall Cocke speaking out at a provincial council meeting and expressing something Yvonne did not agree with. Up at the podium as party president and chair of the meeting, Yvonne put him down by saying, "I don't think so, dear. Don't worry that pretty little head over it." Or words to that effect. The heavy-duty women's rights group loved it, and Cocke probably did as well. But the uncommon differences between Levi and Cocke were the kinds that are repeated endlessly in traditional government regimes with deeply entrenched bureaucracies. It's part of why we were special: we had few self-serving officials whispering in our ears, and most of us got along with each other with great ease.

I got a sense of the alternative when attending cabinet meetings in the early 1990s Harcourt administration, with tons of bureaucrats in the seats around the wall during cabinet meetings. They never missed a nuance, a slight, or I suspect a potential benefit for their role or turf. They saw and heard it all. No bureaucrats—absolutely none—attended cabinet during our first year or more, when we were most productive. And only Eliesen thereafter. Have historians picked up on this? Think of the implications: it empowered *us*, the elected people; and later it empowered Eliesen, but too late for him to be really dangerous (other than setting us up for an election loss, which is another story). Also in those times, the minister appointed our executive assistants, so the executive assistants were loyal to their individual ministers. They didn't report to a deputy in the Office of the Premier. And we also appointed our deputies. So once again, the chain of command was very different from today.

Because the politicians were in control, ministers were not ratted on via a heavily centralized structure. And that was very much Barrett's view. As he said many times in cabinet, "You guys have to understand you're the cabinet's representative in the department, not the department's representative in the cabinet." Barrett always got the fundamentals right; the details were another matter. Once, he told me an American official came up to him and pulled him aside from a crowded gathering to warn him he had some dangerous men inside his cabinet—i.e., far too left. Barrett said, "I told him to just fuck off, I know my people." He was really pleased he'd done that, and did not want to hear any US intelligence gossip. On this issue, Norman Levi kept track of officials coming to BC and where some of them had been in the past.

Let's talk about the office of the speaker in the legislature. We've had many, many speakers and assistant speakers over the years, and only a few stick in the memory. A Social Credit MLA from Prince Rupert, William Harvey Murray, was in the role most of the time I was in Victoria. I recall Walter Davidson from Delta mainly because he was such a rogue and milked it as much as he could. John Reynolds of West Vancouver played the role to the hilt and shared the wealth with the opposition. He also had a secretary in his office who we both got along with very well, which made a huge difference in meeting opposition budget needs. And of course the staffing and budget of the speaker's office ballooned in turn over the years.

The lifestyle of George MacMinn played a huge role in establishing that gravy train. MacMinn was clerk of the House. When I first arrived in Victoria, Ned DeBeck was clerk of the House. Of slight stature but great presence with his thick, long grey hair and thoughtful demeanour, he was truly an ornament in parliament. DeBeck always led an evening seminar at his Victoria home, a comfortable old place, for the new MLAS. This was not an Oak Bay waterfront mansion with a tennis court such as the one his successor MacMinn has lived in for years. DeBeck's seminars were about the basic rules, parliamentary rules, and they were thoughtful, succinct lectures.

Ned DeBeck was a special British Columbian indeed. He'd had a great history on the coast and actually spoke the early trading dialect with the First Nations at the turn of the century, Chinook Wawa. DeBeck also knew the House. He would finish his sessions down in his basement where he had a woodworking shop and turned out beautiful work. When I was one of the new boys elected in 1966, DeBeck presented each of us with his own crafted gift, a beautiful gavel, from "the Office of the Speaker."

DeBeck never worked full time and garnered only a modest salary. After all, W.A.C. Bennett only called the House in January and insisted on getting us out by Easter no matter how many late-night settings he put us through. Like my colleagues, I was exhausted at the end of it. I was a bachelor though, and would escape to San Francisco every spring, read Paul Goodman in a park and...recover. But DeBeck was a treasure. He had two part-time legal assistants—George MacMinn and Ian Horne. They each had their own legal practices as well. Horne had a side job looking after estates under the office of the Public Guardian and Trustee of BC.

MacMinn ran a broader practice, part of which—getting liquor licences approved—was probably a good revenue producer. I later became involved in that aspect through a private interest and of course found it had been a huge area of privilege over the years—finally shifting away from the Province after Bill Vander Zalm got in the game for Peter Toigo. When I hired Rob Evans, the carpenter who built the magnificent new Strathcona Hotel bar on Douglas Street in Victoria, to help me fix up the Railway Club in Vancouver, Evans introduced me to the Strathcona's owner. The owner had an extraordinary number of licences in his establishment. Being in the biz, I asked, "How'd you manage all this anyway?"

His answer: George MacMinn. In one of the Strathcona's renovations, a tennis court was built on the hotel's roof; MacMinn played on it regularly. Later when I checked Speaker Walter Davidson's accounts while labouring on the public accounts committee, I uncovered how much he was spending on booze—and even on aspirin. I was able to say in the House, "We not only paid for the party...We paid for the hangover too." I was also able to find that by the time MacMinn became clerk of the House, we were paying him very handsomely and covering parliamentary gatherings at watering holes around the world. The office had quietly become a burial ground for high spending. In MacMinn's case, he not only obtained a very good salary with pension benefits and maintained a downtown office, but also offered separate consulting to the speaker's office as well. This work presumably involved analyzing rules around the world and coming up with new proposals for BC.

The substantial bills I reviewed for this work included a handwritten notation to take a deduction for the provincial pension he would get as a result of his regular job as clerk. In other words, not only was he getting his own salary as clerk, he was also getting a substantial consulting fee and then he was using the volume of his own consulting fee to top up his government pension. The government contribution for his expanded pension was based on them accepting the idea it was a wage, not a fee. Only with the revelations in 2021 about the Office of the Speaker does the whole province finally realize what a slush bucket that operation has been. Later when I became deputy minister for Crown corporations and saw more of the deputies and their assistant deputies close up, I was awestruck that all too often the driving force for most of these folks was the perks and lifestyle. Victoria is a very nice place for them indeed. No more Ned DeBecks.

But the speaker's office also managed the intern programs with the University of Victoria, a project that introduced political science kids to the actual workings of the House. Some would work for the government caucus, and others would work for the opposition. I was lucky enough to have Richard Bridge work with me. He became a long-time colleague and later joined Crerar and me in the transition work for the Harcourt government. He then worked with us in the Crown corporations secretariat and later worked with me and others on the business plan for Vancity's Regional Development Corporation, which became Vancity Capital Corporation. Bridge continues to do great legal work for NGOs and charitable groups from the Maritimes farm he moved to for his kids' sake.

Chris Catliff was also an intern who worked for me. His father was a judge and his mother, Joyce, was the long-time secretary of the Vancouver City Planning Commission. Joyce had urged young Catliff to work with me should he get the chance. Another intern I spent some time with was Martyn Brown. He became the long-time top political operative for Gordon Campbell in the new premier's office. The most recent work he did was the reorganization of the various resource ministries (land, forestry, mineral, etc.) into one giant shop to service corporate clients—that's what they saw the public lands as being all about. And with that it was the end of the forest service after nearly one hundred years of existence. It will take a fine mind to correct this. The present

Horgan government has now completed their initial work on this question. It remains to be seen if it is adequate for the challenge. My view is that the six or so macro-regions of BC should be the base to work from, each with local people, including Indigenous representatives.

10. OUT OF POWER

It was barely three years after we first took office in the autumn of 1975 that Barrett called an election—an election determined more by Marc Eliesen than anyone, I suspect. We had an upwards blip in the polls as a result of Barrett taking on one of the unions. Eliesen had been in charge of the polling and never provided cabinet or myself with the raw data or analysis that may have illuminated a blip; his reports were always verbal. In cabinet there was a high level of trust between us, especially in the original core group, and we were generous with that trust. It included Eliesen because Barrett trusted Eliesen.

I had been away at a resources ministers' conference in Cape Breton, Nova Scotia (where I had met Wilson Parasiuk and was very impressed; he was deputy premier to Ed Schreyer in Manitoba then). At that conference, I was once again surprised to find how much I was in sync with the Quebecers—so much like us in a policy sense and sharing the same sense of isolation from the feds. By the time I got back, Barrett was ready to go to the people. There were mixed feelings in cabinet and caucus. The crassest view was expressed by Ernest Hall who said, "I can think of 52,000 reasons not to go now" (cabinet ministers at that time were paid $52,000 a year). Barrett was gung-ho, and I was loyal to him. We also assumed Eliesen had good data.

In caucus there were very mixed feelings, with some of the MLAs expressing them quite negatively to the leader. I recall saying to those new kids on the block, "Many of you here got in on the coattails of Dave Barrett. If you shit on those coattails, you're going to slip off." Barrett loved me for that one. But we *were* unprepared; it was just a blip in the polls. Some thought that even so, we had saved ourselves from a more disastrous loss later on. Maybe. We had been in the basement of public opinion for a couple years. Policies like the Agricultural Land Commission and the associated ALR program had engendered Klan-like meetings in agricultural regions throughout the province. And I was the grey eminence behind that.

I had often thought we would be a one-term government, and that's one of the reasons I went at our chance to govern as keenly as I had, doing as much as I could, when I could. Barrett brought back Manny Dunsky for the campaign's public relations, but Dunsky virtually had a breakdown as we moved into the campaign. It was a hell of a mess. I filled in a bit of the gap. With Dunsky, I churned out a one-page newspaper ad with prominent people endorsing us, each in a real, complete way. Most of them were my contacts and supporters: people like Arthur Erickson and Randy Sandner, a sawmill owner at Christina Lake who had been on the board of the Kootenay Boundary Regional District when I was their consulting planner. They were all people I contacted directly; I thought it was a great ad. Many of them paid a handsome price for their support. Arthur Erickson never, ever, got a provincial commission from the Socreds. Grace McCarthy publicly stated that it was because of his endorsement of the NDP. Bing Thom learned a lesson from that one.

The results were grim. We were badly cut back, but not decimated. Barrett, however, was beaten by a small margin in Coquitlam. Opposition caucus meetings were dour. In the early stage, I thought Bill King might be best to take over the reins. Remembering an ancient slogan of Mackenzie King in one of his prime ministerial campaigns, "King or Chaos," I sent a little note to Bill King over the caucus table, asking him to consider it and saying his slogan could be "King *and* Chaos." He was unaware of the previous slogan, unfortunately, and wasn't interested anyway.

A consensus emerged fairly quickly that Barrett should run in a by-election. Eileen Dailly made it clear she would be prepared to give up her North Burnaby seat for Barrett. I and others argued she should be provided with funds to handle what might be a difficult transition.

We all agreed. Barrett indicated after private sessions with Stupich that the Nanaimo Commonwealth Holding Society could provide those funds. But it became apparent very soon, to me at least, that Dailly was wandering about in a ghostlike state and seemed most unwell.

I said to Barrett, "Hell, I can handle a break, and it's time Alex retired." (Vancouver East was a two-member riding at that time.) "I can run in his place in the next election. In the meantime, I can work as a caucus advisor," I suggested. Barrett was keen and said, "Yes, that's what we'll do, and later we'll get rid of Alex." I worked in the by-election for Barrett. It was a triumphant trip down memory lane for Barrett in his old neighbourhood. Franco Cuzetto, one of our most devout, delightful members, accompanied Barrett to what seemed like hundreds of coffee parties. It was a fun campaign and Barrett did well.

I moved into a small office in the caucus rooms near Barrett and undertook my work there. All too soon it became clear that me being so close was a constant reminder to Barrett of his loss and failure. My presence as a staffer in his office was an anchor that dragged him down. So I decided that moving to Vancouver was my best bet. I could look after the riding and consult directly with the party and the caucus. Lea and I found a great house at 2397 Wall Street, not far from our old place, and placed Suzanne in Sir William Macdonald Elementary near Victoria Drive, which I thought was a calculated risk—it's a very tough neighbourhood. But she took to it well, experienced the wonderful diversity of the East Side, and moreover, I suspect, grew tougher than if we'd located elsewhere. Around grade three we went to a school play—*Snow White and the Seven Dwarfs*. Almost everyone was Asian, including Snow White.

I continued working for the caucus, the party and of course the riding, where I continued to be president right until running again. It was during this period that the Pearse Royal Commission on Forest Resources reported out. I carried out a very substantial review of the report for caucus and worked with the forestry critic, my friend Bill King. A year later when the new Forest Act was brought forward, I carried out a detailed review. Sessions were held with various citizen groups and I provided recommendations to King, Barrett and caucus. During these years, I also sat on the provincial executive of the NDP and was invited to speak around the province by various NDP constituency groups. I spoke to various academic groups as well.

My loyal friends in Vancouver East were determined that I would come back to the legislature in Victoria. We were all rooted there and shared a side of the class divide that Alex Macdonald did not share. So prior to the 1979 election, I ran for the nomination against Macdonald. Barrett never lived up to our clear agreement when I resigned. I think what he said to me was something like, "You know, Bob, there are not friendships in politics; there are shifting coalitions and allegiances." Barrett was in the telephone war rooms calling for our folks to support Macdonald. The nominating meeting was at Vancouver Technical Secondary School auditorium. It was a huge crowd, and Macdonald won. By that point I almost hoped for that result because I didn't think we'd be able to win the election and I might be blamed if I were a candidate.

I continued to actively work in the riding and when it became clear to Barrett that he was not doing so well, he resigned, and there was another by-election in Vancouver East in 1984. My loyal wonderful friends, including Glen Clark, saw to it that I won. I had known Clark since he was eighteen years old, and he would soon join me as an MLA in the two-member riding when Macdonald retired in the next general election.

Over the time I was out of the legislature, I had also determined I should use my entrepreneurial skills learned while acquiring forest companies for the benefit my family, and also for the community. I realized I should start having fun. I realized, "Okay, I can't peddle myself as a planner anymore in this province, because I'm only seen as a politician." So I thought I'd better get into business. I was a bit of a romantic about pubs and inns and meeting places, and started looking at the economics of beer parlours. I concluded they were a terrific buy, because the price was usually based on cash flow and the underlying real estate wasn't part of the analysis. You had an underlying guarantee of a strong real

Bob with Nelly (left) and Aunt Kay Williams (right) at the Barnet Motor Inn, a motel and
lounge in Port Moody, BC, that Bob acquired as a family business in the 1980s. Bob Williams
Collection

estate base below a substantial cash flow. And I could actually buy some
of the places I was looking at in downtown Vancouver. I made an offer
on a pub near Georgia and Richards, but the guy walked away from the
deal. I could have sued him, but didn't.

In 1979, we acquired a small hotel in Port Moody, the Barnet Motor
Inn, and ran it as a family business. It became quite successful. It was of
post-war construction, though not one of the oldies, with about twenty
rooms and a large beer parlour and lounge. I had a lot of fun with it. I
had renovated a lot of housing in my side jobs, so was able to renovate
the beer parlour. It became a really interesting space, the country music
hall for all the suburbs. I started realizing that the business was essentially an entertainment business. We even had the remnants of the old
loggers from skid row who would come and leave a roll of money in the
vault with Lea and say, "Warn me a week before the money starts running out." It was just like classic early days in the Downtown Eastside. A

logger would hook up with his favourite prostitute and shack up for two weeks, then finally learn the money was running out. It was a wonderful education about that world.

After running the Barnet Motor Inn for a few years, we bought the Railway Club on Dunsmuir Street in downtown Vancouver. It had been founded as the Railwaymen's Club in the 1930s, a private club for railway workers who were barred from the nearby exclusive Engineers' Club. It was later operated as a gambling saloon by a very interesting woman, Dagny Forslund. Before starting renovations, I did a tour down the west coast, doing my own analysis of what makes a good bar. On the basis of our learnings from that less-than-sober tour, I designed the Railway Club to look like it had always been an old bar. It hadn't; we made it look like that.

It soon became a serious entertainment centre for live music, which we pioneered with k.d. lang and other significant artists. It was a new education and new demographic for me. The club became a centre for poets and authors and actors. And it was the favourite watering hole after a gig for bands like Spirit of the West and the Tragically Hip.

The Railway Club, a bar that Bob purchased, refurbished and operated in Downtown Vancouver from the 1980s to 2000s. Bob Williams Collection

John Mann and his gang at Spirit of the West wrote a wonderful song about the Railway Club that goes something like, "I know a little place you might not have found. It looks down on the city from the underground." The club established a reputation across Canada. We had it for almost thirty years. Our daughter Janet managed Spirit of the West for over ten years while at the same time being the de facto boss of the Railway Club.

Building on that base in the entertainment industry, we ran similar family businesses over the years, most recently Sisto's, a neighbourhood pub in Mission in the Fraser Valley, which my youngest daughter, Suzanne, managed. I also began my long tenure as a director and advisor at Vancity Credit Union along with short part-time teaching stints both at UBC in community and regional planning, and at Simon Fraser University's business school on Crown corporations and public policy.

I returned to politics when Barrett stepped down as leader and Vancouver East MLA in 1984. I felt great loyalty to the riding and to my friends there. I had also developed a good capacity to take on the government, beat the hell out of them in question periods and find out where the main opportunities were for dealing with their weaknesses. I felt the party needed my skill, and was ready and willing to go back. Shortly after I won the by-election and returned to the legislature, I was again elected chair of the NDP caucus in Victoria.

In the leadership race triggered by Barrett's resignation, I supported Bill King. But there was a division in the party, essentially between the Barrett gang, many of whom supported King, and the Dennis Cocke gang who supported the former deputy minister to the attorney general, David Vickers. He was an excellent candidate, and an excellent person, and he might very well have won us government. But Bob Skelly came up the middle and won on the fifth ballot. (Vickers later became a provincial Supreme Court judge.)

I worked hard for Skelly during the time he was leader, and helped cover a lot of gaps in the caucus. Reluctantly, I finally came to the conclusion that he was emotionally incapable of running in the election, and more and more of the caucus had come to the same conclusion. I suppose I was the leader of the group that thought we had to let Skelly go. I checked with people who were close to Mike Harcourt and asked if he was ready to assume that role if we quickly got rid of Skelly. Harcourt indicated yes, as long as there were no fingerprints. We had the numbers to remove Skelly the night before a caucus meeting a few months before the election. But some of the people who had agreed didn't come to the meeting. Alex Macdonald and Frank Mitchell, the MLA from Esquimalt, who had both agreed that Skelly had to go, did not show up. So we didn't have the votes. Skelly fell apart in his first interview of that election, which some of us had predicted would happen.

We lost the election in 1986 and Skelly stepped down. There was unanimity that Harcourt was the guy to replace Skelly, and Harcourt won the subsequent leadership convention by acclamation. I think the truth was a lot of us thought Harcourt could be managed. Some of us saw him as a liberal who didn't have experience in Victoria. The flaw with that line of thinking is that when people have the job, they have the job. I think there were unrealistic expectations in terms of how that period would go under Harcourt's leadership.

In the legislature prior to the election in 1986, I hammered the Socred regime on corrupt land deals, as I had done previously. My shadow critic roles through those years included forestry, environment and economic development. Vaughn Palmer did a lot of reporting on that and the kind of role I played being the mean son of a bitch on the other side of the House. I played a very substantial role in grinding the government down, contributing to the Socreds' decision to ditch Bill Bennett on the eve of that election and replace him with Vander Zalm.

During our time in government, I developed a plan for the Central Coast that would open up access to the forest lands that were under-allocated to fortify employment in Ocean Falls, Bella Bella and Bella Coola. This included a subregional plan to build a road over the hump to Roscoe Inlet from Ocean Falls, which would then readily link Bella Bella with Ocean Falls and Bella Coola with a small ferry service.

I saw it as the beginnings of a small ferry service on the coast, dropping people off near Bella Coola and then linking through to the Chilcotin. It would open up the Central Coast as it had never been opened up before. Then we reviewed the wood tenders to determine the amount of unallocated timber.

I helicoptered the region up to Kimsquit River in the northern channel between Bella Coola and Ocean Falls—a magnificent valley. I happened to helicopter up there in the time of the salmon run, and there were thousands of eagles in the air as we flew amongst them. It was like being at the beginning of time on this coast in the pristine magnificence of it all. I thought to myself, if we're going to develop this area, let's do it on a more modest scale and have it benefit the small communities here on the coast. It would be an incremental exercise. So I determined that there would be modest and focused industrial development to keep the communities alive and involved in the region, while limiting the overall ecological impact.

After we were defeated in 1975, the Socreds closed down Ocean Falls and the tenure that was going to be made available on the Kimsquit River came up for grabs under the Bill Bennett government. Bennett had an association with Herb Doman, a lumber boss from Duncan. Doman proposed delivering a new pulp mill in Nanaimo as part of getting the Kimsquit tenure. Then he moved in and logged on the Kimsquit valley on a huge scale, apparently with no intention of ever building the envisioned pulp mill. He gutted this magnificent place that I had seen a few years earlier. A local forester sent me the data and pictures. It was disastrous.

I gave speeches in the legislature about this place now becoming "the valley of the moon," in terms of what had happened under Doman. What he did was have Japanese freighters at the mouth of the Kimsquit River taking out raw logs, so the entire valley was gutted to feed Doman's lack of capital. Doman never did deliver the capital product that had justified the tenure: the pulp mill. He did the same thing out on the west coast of Vancouver Island, with yet another a huge tenure. Doman threatened to sue me.

It wasn't until later that we became aware there really was an association between Doman and Bennett. One of our greatest lawyers in the province, Joe Arvay, who moved from the attorney general's office into private practice, went after Bennett for inside trading knowledge around Doman, and won the case. That long linkage between Bennett and Doman was confirmed. But it was too late for the Central Coast and saving Ocean Falls. It's been a constant in this province, right back to Robert Sommers and BC Forest Products. The sweet irony of it all is that sometimes the politician gets caught and goes to jail, as was the case with Sommers. But nobody ever pursued BC Forest Products, who were the people that gave him the money.

I was re-elected in Vancouver East in 1986—my final election campaign, it turned out—and I continued to serve as chair of the NDP caucus under Harcourt's leadership. I was very active in managing caucus affairs as chair, in liaison with the party and dealing with other caucus groups in the legislature. In that role, I convinced Premier Vander Zalm to change the system of governance of the affairs of the members and to bring in a bill to create a Board of Internal Economy to jointly manage these matters. I subsequently served on that board for several years.

Reflecting on my years in the legislature, I find I have very fond memories of the terrific women in the dining room who served us all so well. One might assume that these women were not very political, but that assumption would have been very wrong. Egle and Italia, two sisters down there, were always a pleasure and reflected the generosity of spirit I have happily learned to expect from Italian friends and acquaintances. And being Italian, these women had a natural affinity for the left. The other women universally proved to be simpatico and shared our losses and our occasional victories. The early Socreds apparently had treated them poorly all too often, so that reinforced their feelings.

The great joy amongst the group for me was Jo, a middle-aged stocky woman of Irish background. She never missed a nuance, either upstairs or downstairs. While pouring my regular coffee, she might whisper a comment to me that indicated she fully understood our game and figured out the players and likely implications. After I left the House and saw her soon after, when I was working on the Harcourt transition, she confided to me quietly while the dining room was empty, "When you left, it was like they removed a giant oak from that assembly." It was the highest praise.

It was a morning just like any other when we were all engaged at the legislature that I'd left our offices to pick up a coffee at the old CNIB kiosk just outside the east entrance to the legislature. I was in the line-up ahead of a Socred appointee, who saw me and asked me a question with a double meaning. I responded, "Okay," picked up my coffee and started to head off. He repeated the question then laughed. It was then I recognized the key code word. In effect, he was saying, "I know you're gay." By then my back was to him and he was out of there. I knew they knew I had a gay side, and did not know how they might use it against me. But I'd seen what happened to others. I concluded that I should resign before the next election, and I did.

11. SUPER BUREAUCRAT: WITH THE NDP
GOVERNMENT IN THE 1990S

I was still deeply involved in politics even after I bowed out of my role as an MLA, and was keen to try a bureaucratic role. Prior to the 1991 provincial election, I was chairman of the transition team for the leader of the opposition, Mike Harcourt, which was a big job. In addition to recruiting people, I prepared some papers, including one on the governance of Crown corporations. The team was an excellent group that I played quite a role in choosing. I was able to bring in youngsters like University of Victoria law professor Andrew Petter, who wasn't even an MLA at that stage (he would be elected in 1991 as the new MLA for Saanich South). It was a good, solid committee, with people like George Ford, an immensely able senior bureaucrat from the Prairies who became deputy to the premier.

Heading into summer, I planned on spending a lot of time on Hornby Island—which is a magical place—using my new studio to write about the transition and what I had in mind for the Crown corporations secretariat. I still have a ton of those notes on the transition for the Harcourt government. I was lucky in that Linda Baker (the daughter of Rae Eddie, an early New Westminster MLA) was Harcourt's chief of staff, and would likely hold him to a deal that included me in the Crown corporations role.

After chairing the transition committee and preparing my own detailed notes on the Crown corporations secretariat, we were all ready. I attended the small, happy private party with Harcourt right after the election night when the Socreds were relegated to the dustbin of history. We all had a bit to drink. I was in a big armchair and Baker jumped into my lap, snuggled up to me, kissed me on the cheek, and whispered, "It's

Bob tends the garden at his cottage on Hornby Island, BC, c. 1990. Bob Williams Collection

done. You'll be heading up the Crown corporations secretariat." It came as a great relief, as there had always been a slight coolness between me and Harcourt. It was never a rupture, but he was a pretty conventional liberal, really, and if I wasn't a man in the tradition of the European Social Democrats, I was one hell of a *Red* Tory. We had offices for our team in the courthouse in Vancouver. Ironically, it was behind one of the waterfalls, as when Erickson was designing Robson Square and we were looking at his work, I said, "Arthur, you're famous for your leaky roofs, and you're putting a lake and a waterfall on this bloody roof." I was able to work under it for a couple of weeks, frustrated by the noise.

This time, the interregnum was fascinating. Political scientists should really look at these critical moments of change in history. I had a team of about a dozen people reviewing all the briefing books prepared by the public service for each minister. It was a hell of a job to go through it all, reviewing all dossiers and seeing what we thought was valid and invalid, and what we thought the priorities were compared to the civil servants. The biggest issues were complications around BC Rail and Northeast Coal. Fortunately, a top economist civil servant, Frank Blasetti, was on the case and was invaluable as we untangled the mess for the new minister of transportation, Art Charbonneau. It was about ten days of intensive work for our crew—a far, far cry from Barrett and I having lunch at the Only Cafe on Hastings nineteen years earlier in 1972!

It was fascinating to hear the loud noises from people banging on our door, insisting on access. The worst one was a senior official, an engineer, insisting on some major capital expenditure decision for rapid transit. Those types were all moved to the end of the line. The ones with judgment and smarts kept their distance and didn't respond until they were asked. And the transition team more or less set the agenda for the first few months.

I became a deputy minister and secretary of the cabinet committee on Crown corporations, which was then headed by the able young Minister Glen Clark, who also served as minister of finance. I also headed the newly established Crown corporations secretariat in the Ministry of Finance, and proceeded to hire assistant deputy ministers and staff. I carried out that role for two years. In many ways, serving as Crown deputy was a more substantial responsibility than being a cabinet minister. I leaped into the new position with Alistair Crerar, my old mentor from planning school; Richard Bridge, who had previously worked with me as an executive assistant; Marvin Shaffer, a brilliant PhD economist who was strong on energy and hydro, an area I needed help in; and Robyn Allan. Shaffer was a wonderful asset who I'd only got to know during the transition interregnum. We were a great team, even if Harcourt never got it. His deputy George Ford did, and was a thoughtful ally. Prior to the establishment of the Crown corporations secretariat, there had not been a central overview of the Crowns, and there had not been centrally determined initiatives either. Among the achievements of the secretariat were:

- adequate monitoring of ICBC rates;
- some forty million in savings for BC Rail in the Northeast Coal bankruptcy;
- establishing the Columbia Basin Trust and sharing of power benefits with the region;
- establishing a rate of return on capital employed at BC Hydro, and new dividends for the Crown;
- establishing peak pricing systems for BC Ferries, to begin to relate to capital demands for capacity in the peak summer season;
- advancing the concept of aluminum fast ferries for the BC Ferries system;
- carrying out the initial work analysis and proposals for the West Coast Express, the commuter rail that now serves the communities on the north side of the river to Mission;
- developing the Victoria Accord, a joint agreement between the Province and the City of Victoria to redevelop the Legislative Precinct, rehabilitate St. Ann's Academy, plan the distribution of government buildings, establish a new ferry terminal and port management, and a local streetcar system;
- working jointly with the Land Title Office, BC Assessment Authority, property transfer tax office staff and BC Buildings Corporation to prepare a property management, land title and local tax system for the City of St. Petersburg, Russia;
- working with BC Rail to establish a provincially owned long-distance telephone carrier that would use their fibre-optic line

and coordinating with BC Transit, BC Hydro and other Crown agencies with fibre-optic capacity to deliver communication services with Westel Communications, a wholly owned subsidiary, being the successful result (until being sold off during the Campbell government's fire sale of public assets in 2002);

- working with BC Rail to get into the port and rail businesses, with an ill-managed private company, Vancouver Wharves, acquired and enhanced much to the relief of bulk shippers and the Port of Vancouver; and

- regularly reviewing of capital spending, and the business plans of all Crown corporations.

While we achieved much during my time as deputy minister of Crown corporations, there were limits to how far my political masters were prepared to go. I was thwarted from acquiring the Roberts Bank coal terminal as an asset for BC Rail, which was then headed by its most able CEO, Paul McElligott. Harcourt backed off because Jimmy Pattison wanted it and it is now Pattison's most valuable asset.

The new government also bowed to the province's corporate power elite in other ways. One of Glen Clark's first actions as minister of finance was letting Doman be overcompensated for his licences in the Charlottes (Haida Gwaii) when they went into the national park. We had had Richard Schwindt, an immensely capable economist at SFU, advise us on compensation of forest companies when we took back their licences. He had rightly recommended they only be compensated for capital, not the Crown land they never paid for. That was a rule both Williston and I, during our times as ministers, religiously applied. Sorry, Glen, you shouldn't have done it.

One of my proudest achievements as deputy minister of Crown corporations was the creation of the Columbia Basin Trust, a capstone to the unfinished business from my earlier work as minister in the 1970s. The travesty of the giveaway of the Kootenay River dam sites to Cominco— which my loyal deputy minister Valter Raudsepp had shared with me all those years ago—stuck with me. In my role as minister responsible for BC Hydro, I had looked for ways to harness the great potential of the Columbia and its tributaries for the benefit of the people of the Kootenay region.

Some preliminary work in this direction had occurred through some creative adjustments to the BC Hydro board of directors. W.A.C. Bennett had kept a small board, the key person being the minister, Ray Williston and the chair, Gordon Shrum. A former physics professor at UBC, Shrum was famous for moving the wartime army barracks from Little Mountain to UBC to handle the massive post-war influx of students, as well as for initiating SFU. There was also a quiet, long-time BC Hydro engineer on the board, Jack Steede, who was called an executive director. It became clear early in the game that Steede was highly qualified in his engineering field, and housed a fine corporate memory of the workings of our most important utility. I concluded we should keep him on the board.

Shrum, who I had also contacted during the interregnum in the 1970s, had come to see me at my somewhat ramshackle East Side home on Wall Street to provide me with background information I requested on the Kootenay Canal project. Nothing could have defined the end of a regime so much as Shrum climbing up the steep back steps of our old home, entering at the back door, pushing off our German shepherd, Fritz, removing his homburg in the kitchen and advising, "Honourable Minister, I have brought the material you requested." I invited the chairman into the living room. We had a short talk, thanked each other and then he headed downstairs to a waiting limousine. Our neighbourhood had not seen a limo since the week I was acting mayor in the midsixties, when it came into the hood to take the local kids for a ride and a tour of the Vancouver Aquarium just before Christmas. To my mind, Shrum was too closely identified with the previous administration to keep on, able as he was.

The role of executive director at BC Hydro under our watch seemed to be a natural fit for my former professor and mentor Jim Wilson. Wilson had been the executive director of the Lower Mainland Regional Planning Board when I worked there as a summer student, and he had taught planning at UBC. In earlier days, he had worked as an engineer at the renowned Tennessee Valley Authority, an enormous project out of the Roosevelt administration of the 1930s. He was also a planning graduate from the eminent University of North Carolina at Chapel Hill. It made sense for Wilson to be a full-time executive director at BC Hydro, and I expected him to play a major role focusing on environmental concerns. At last we could have an environmental watchdog within BC Hydro.

I had felt the need for environmental oversight at BC Hydro from my days hiking as a kid near Stave Lake, north of Mission, where no clearing of the forest had occurred prior to flooding. I later felt the need even more so when flying over the devastation at Williston Lake, the giant reservoir behind the W.A.C. Bennett Dam on the Peace River. The destruction up there seemed endless. The more I got to know about the process that determined the go-ahead on the Peace, the more I realized how inadequate it had been. I was overjoyed when Wilson agreed to come back home from the University of Waterloo with Renate and his three boys to British Columbia. Wilson became executive director of BC Hydro.

It was a special plus having Wilson at Hydro because he had been in charge of resettlement in the Arrow Lakes pursuant to the flooding under the Columbia River Treaty. Wilson had written of his concerns about the resettlement on the Columbia in an important little book entitled *People in the Way*. He said, "Look. Yes, we paid them. Yes, they've been compensated. But we destroyed their whole lifestyle. There's a bigger obligation we have to them." As deputy of Crowns in the Harcourt government, I owed it to the people of the region, and to Wilson, to follow through with the Columbia Basin Trust. Sometimes it takes that long for important proposals to gel. Often time, knowledge, experience and a dose of wisdom is the necessary recipe.

My assistant deputy minister Marvin Shaffer and another brilliant staffer, Bruce Duncan, took the idea of the trust and ran with it along with Lorne Sivertson, another top staffer. The trust was also a goal of the unique MLA from Nelson–Creston, Corky Evans. The idea of sharing the rent of a river with the people of the region that the river flowed through was a new twist on the thoughts of the early great American economist Henry George. It was, in my mind's eye, to become the means for the people of the Columbia Basin to move up the learning curve that I and others had had the privilege to travel; learning to balance between environment and the economy, and using revenues to enhance a people and their region in economic, social, educational and cultural ways. We all shared in the rent of the river. It was real empowerment. It was in the 1990s that I took the idea to the Crown corporations committee of cabinet. As chair of the committee, Glen Clark asked, "If we do this on the Columbia, won't they want it in other regions and other rivers in the province?"

I replied, with a gleam in my eye, "I hope so, Minister." Clark laughed. The light dawned. We were talking about a real transfer of power to the people of the regions. Since undertaking that change, and viewing the great success of the Columbia Basin Trust ever since, I have been completely convinced about the need to transfer power away from Victoria to our grand macro-regions. I saw it as a longer-term game involving other natural resources, so that the natural next step would be forests. To have forests and water essentially sent off to the macro-regions strikes me as the important way to manage the future of this province. Another obvious macro-region is Vancouver Island.

A joint agreement had been signed between BC Trade Development Corporation, BC Assessment Authority, Land Titles Branch of the attorney general's office, BC Buildings Corporation and the BC Systems Corporation to work toward preparation of a master plan for managing the real estate of the City of St. Petersburg, Russia, a city of over six million people, blessed with some ten thousand heritage buildings. There was in turn an agreement with the Property Committee of City Council of St. Petersburg (a new legislature of some four hundred members), the deputy mayor for property and the St. Petersburg Property Fund to carry out the initial analysis and plan. I chaired and led the BC team on the project. And after my two years with the Crown corporations secretariat, I continued on the St. Petersburg project through the BC Trade Development Corporation.

The proposal was most ambitious, but the opportunity was enormous! The Western world barely comprehends how great the shift of wealth is in these post-Communist societies. Our plans involved the establishment of a land registry, a property management capacity at the civic level, a property tax system, a computer system in relation to the whole project, a property transfer tax and a training program—all in a business plan framework. We did get some federal Canadian support and prepared a comprehensive, exciting business plan for the Russians. We even had enthusiastic support from the Canadian ambassador to Russia.

In reality, however, BC cannot compete for any significant federal support in areas like international consulting support against entrenched interests in Ontario and even more so in Quebec. So even though the BC Torrens system of land title is far superior to anything in Quebec or Ontario, the politics of the country favour eastern Canada. Similarly, our property assessment and tax system are amongst the best in North America, but so what? The other rock we bashed against in the end was corruption and mafia in Russia, which is endemic. The modest reformer we worked with in St. Petersburg was shot by a mafia sniper from a rooftop on Nevsky Prospect, the main street.

For me, it was as exciting as anything I have ever worked on. It is an area BC has great expertise in, and we barely realize it. Had we been able to pursue the plan we laboured over, we would have immensely improved the quality of life in St. Petersburg. The final work on the St. Petersburg project ended in early 1995. In the fall of 1994, USAID arrived in St. Petersburg with copious "free money" and an American ideological view of the world. A much less ambitious program was pursued, and the prospect of any real sharing of the city's great urban land wealth with all of its citizens disappeared.

While the project was still underway, we had calculated the land rents along Nevsky Prospect. Our analysis indicated the land rents would be equal to most of the great cities in Europe. We shared with the

Russians the system of land ownership and rent in the City of Westminster in London, UK, where you have incredible cash flow land rent from the heart of the city. It got so substantial over time that they were able to fund the National Trust and all the great estates and castles in Great Britain. We were trying to convince the Russians to apply that model in St. Petersburg. With reforms toward democratization and distributing the land rent, there was enormous potential. If you can capture the rent of great cities, it's the ultimate democracy (something Henry George would argue).

But it was not to be. During those crazy years as the changes in Russia occurred they had re-established a civic government in St. Petersburg. It was bigger than our legislature, and the people in that city council were excellent, genuine democrats and reformers. But the people of Russia got disenchanted very quickly with this idea of democracy. The turnouts for city council elections were so modest, and under their rules if the turnout was too low, then the election result was null and void. So the whole council became null and void! In the middle of our work there, we went from working with a democratic city council to a bureaucracy that was tied, no, chained to Moscow. It was the Communist apparatus, a gangster-led apparatus, and it became an overt one linked with the mafia after the change. The land rent in the cities became the cash flow for the mafia.

In St. Petersburg, I got insight into the workings of bureaucracy, and I began to understand an apparatchik's mind. At a meeting with all the bureaucrats in St. Petersburg, to implement a land registry and local governance system, I tried to talk to them about inventory, analysis, plans and processes. It became clear to me that they didn't know what the word *analysis* meant, which was a huge kick in the head. Another time, coming in on the taxi bus from the Moscow airport into the centre of town, I looked at the poverty and misery and said to myself, "How the hell did American intelligence ever convince the West that this animal was the danger that they claimed it was?" It was clearly a monstrous third-tier country, where it had an abusive, empty-headed system. For a person of the moderate left in the West to see the reality of the Stalinist world was a hell of a shock. And to find that their bureaucrats virtually had had lobotomies, so that post-1917 they didn't have the ability to analyze anything, or were punished if they did, was shocking, too.

In 1998, I was appointed by the Glen Clark government to serve as chair of the Insurance Corporation of British Columbia (ICBC), the government insurance company that we had started during our time in government in the 1970s. Andrew Petter had been given the ministerial responsibility for ICBC. They were looking for somebody to chair the corporation and the headhunter had recommended the usual right-wing corporate types, which Petter wasn't happy with. So it crossed his mind: "Why don't I get Bob Williams to do this?" I served as chair of ICBC until Gordon Campbell and his Liberals took power in 2001.

The highlight of my work as chair of the ICBC board was the creation of the Surrey Central City project—which transformed North Surrey. With the support of the board, and leveraging the corporation's $6 billion in reserves, I was able to get the project underway during my tenure as chair. This transformational project revitalized the land use and economic pattern of North Surrey while also creating an opportunity to expand access to post-secondary students south of the Fraser River. A new technical university became an anchor of the project, establishing a new Surrey campus at the Central City.

Where did the Central City project come from? I had been working with Bing Thom on the question of a new university in Surrey. At the time, the Province was pursuing the idea of building a university around Cloverdale, which was in the middle of nowhere. Thom and I came to the conclusion that any university should be in Whalley, which is the nominal centre of Surrey, even though it was something of a suburban, commercial slum. Shortly after I was appointed chair of ICBC, Andrew Petter's responsibilities shifted, and he became minister of advanced education. These activities all merged at the same time. Thom and I convinced Petter that any new university should be right at the main SkyTrain station in the new town centre of Surrey, to renovate what was a commercial slum. Bob Strachan, the founder of ICBC, had convinced me that using the reserves in insurance companies was an enormous opportunity for rebuilding British Columbia itself, rather than just investing in paper in Toronto or New York. So the first thing I wanted to look at with ICBC was what we did with our reserves. I became convinced about transforming North Surrey.

To my mind, North Surrey was the new East Side in the metropolitan region. It desperately needed funding and a transformation—a point never understood by civil servants in Victoria. North Surrey also had most of the kids in the region, and that would continue to be so in the long run. So the idea of having a university right at their main transit junction would show local kids they had a potentially different future; that was a big part of how I looked at it. There was a lacklustre, substantial shopping centre right near the SkyTrain station that was for sale, so I acquired it through ICBC with the idea that we would transform it into a new city centre. And I hired a pro to manage the project, Gordon Paul Smith, who had worked for Jimmy Pattison on Expo and had done projects with Thom in Madrid and elsewhere. (I managed the project myself for several months before realizing it was a gargantuan task that must be transferred to a professional.)

My executive assistant at the time, Monica Hay (later Monica Morgan), was invaluable as we carpentered through, shifting from consultants to our own corporate entity with Gordon Paul Smith. During that time, she developed great skill in managing complex projects and has since worked on Vancouver's major new St. Paul's Hospital and other large developments. With her early guidance and Gordon Paul Smith's know-how, the Surrey project came in ahead of time and under budget. It was a transformational project. We invested $250 million, redesigning the shopping centre to create the university and tower for a new ICBC headquarters and a galleria.

The new government tried to get rid of it when they were elected in 2001. But the project had advanced so far so fast that when the new chair of ICBC went to Smith and said, "We'd like to stop the project. Can you do that?" Smith wisely said, "Yes, of course. It will cost you more to stop it than to finish it. But the decision is yours." Smith is a very smart fellow and he'd built up an enormous inventory to complete the project. The mayor of Surrey Dianne Watts subsequently said that our work generated $4 billion in private investment soon afterwards, and now that just keeps multiplying. We had been attacked at the time for investing $250 million. Bob Bose, an earlier mayor of Surrey, asked the critics, "Are you saying it's too good for Surrey?" It won all the international prizes, the best awards in Cannes.

A few years later, Andrew Petter was appointed president of SFU. I put forward the idea to Petter and Joe Segal to expand SFU in Surrey from their campus in our new Central City project. It was basically to branch out in linear ways from the centre, more or less radially, and really cross King George Boulevard, ideally near 102 Avenue but maybe to the north. Bing Thom was wrong about turning his back on the King George—a rare misstep. We need to celebrate it, that ugly highway. Like Las Vegas—celebrate the strip! But we wouldn't go that far. The mix of Bing Thom, Gordon Smith and myself did what most people thought

Bob at the Surrey Central City development, which he advanced as chair of the board of the Insurance Corporation of BC, helping create an urban heart for the sprawling municipality, c. 2016. Bob Williams Collection

impossible—an appealing, exciting central business district south of the river. The truth is the Greater Vancouver Region has been a binodal region, formerly downtown Vancouver and downtown New Westminster linked by the early interurban railway from Carrall Street in Vancouver to Columbia Street in New West, continuing through the valley.

New engineering buildings for SFU have been added to the Central City as well as the new City Hall, the amazing fifty-two-storey hotel and Kwantlen Polytechnic University on the main plaza. In the last provincial election, a second medical university was promised for the next stage of the campus. This new project pioneered by a Crown corporation was finally being seen for the success it was. But it was also pushing us to see the other enormous urban land opportunities in that part of the region. Our bold work of investing ICBC resources in the region has truly paid off. Gordon Smith went on to become the CEO for the newly formed Surrey City Development Corporation followed by Michael Heeney, who had been number two for Bing Thom while their firm was designing the project.

Despite the obvious history of huge new land values related to infrastructure, the Province appears to be blind to the reasonable idea of buying this land early or taxing it substantially in order to share the rent. The money to build the new infrastructure comes from one set of taxpayers, the average folk, and the benefit of huge new rental values falls to the adjacent landowners who never contributed to the cost of the bridge or infrastructure. The Evergreen Extension of the SkyTrain was seen as such a possibility by provincial staff at the time of that project, but the concept was not pursued. Since then, private buyers acquired the Lougheed Mall at North Road and are again in a rezoning process for new condos and rental towers as part of the expanding Lougheed City proposal—another opportunity lost by the builders of the infrastructure.

The tragedy with our ICBC project that has created a new downtown for Surrey was that with the change in government, some seventeen additional acres that the city was ready to option to us as the developer was lost—potentially billions in return. In turn, the new government sold off the shopping centre, galleria and tower we had developed from scratch and left about a billion dollars on the table for the new owners in the form of remaining development rights. All these potential revenues were let go too soon, a lesson for future governments to take a longer view and thus achieve a serious long-term payback. Indeed, there is a need to look at all infrastructure in terms of long-term payback and returns—generating direct revenues for the Crown.

Surrey continues to be a place that deserves government attention in this regard. There is a powerful case to be made for government to reap the return from lands adjacent to new infrastructure, land-use changes, new densities and rezoning. Even now, with the construction of the new Pattullo Bridge between New Westminster and Scott Road, the land values out there will take another leap. Scott Road Station represents an area of likely great increases in land value or rent and the ugly Scott Road junkyard strip, while being heavily contaminated with complicated stability because of soil conditions, is still bound to be the beneficiary of the huge new value of the bridge infrastructure.

For too long, Whalley's Corner—the old name for the Surrey downtown—was ignored, but in many ways other nearby areas have been ignored and haven't been seen as integrated parts of a whole or thought of in a comprehensive way. These are areas where infrastructure keeps being piled on infrastructure in a single-purpose way, rather than in an integrated way, and without consideration of how to optimize the financial relations. For example, the South Fraser Perimeter Road linking Roberts Bank to Port Kells was never seen as the significant piece of infrastructure it is; it was sliced through twenty miles of riverfront without consolidating new development opportunities.

The belly of the region straddles the Fraser River with the old village of Fraser Mills (a convenient tax-limited enclave below Maillardville, in what is now Coquitlam), Bridgeview in North Surrey and the Pattullo Bridge near the Scott Road SkyTrain station, Brownsville and the new North Surrey sport complex. All these scattered pieces can become a new whole with a potential centrality for that part of the Lower Mainland. Another exciting prospect with similarly positive urban and economic impact might well be the Cascadia High Speed Rail proposal potentially linking our region through to Seattle, Portland and possibly even California. This belly of the region would follow the existing Burlington Northern line, replacing the Blaine crossing farther east and crossing into Canada near Cloverdale.

Intriguing indeed is the situation in White Rock, right at the border. White Rock has one of the finest beaches in the region, but its use is constrained terribly because of the Burlington Northern right of way that limits access to the beach in a serious way. The commercial strip on the north side of the shoreline's major road is also terribly constrained and parking is very difficult. There is an enormous opportunity to relocate the rail line inland and fill in a narrow one-block strip for a waterfront downtown for White Rock. The new land values on the waterfront along with a new beach a few miles long would be transformational for the commuters south of the Fraser.

The new land values that would be created on that shoreline would potentially generate an enormous revenue boost, which could help cover costs of rail relocation and new road construction, generating long-term annual returns for any infrastructure agency that might be created for the project, or to share with the City of White Rock itself as the host beach community. Properly conceived and directed, such a White Rock shoreline renewal project might well be the most significant urban project in BC.

12. BANKING FOR THE PEOPLE: CO-OPERATIVE ECONOMICS AT VANCITY CREDIT UNION

The modern Vancity story occurred about thirty-plus years ago when two colleagues and I created what was in fact the beginning of the Action Slate. We knew we needed a three-person slate to run for the three director roles that came up every year. And so the three candidates were Mary Rawson, Jo-Anne Lee and me. I had name recognition from my years as an MLA and got elected, while my colleagues did well but did not quite make it. The following year Gloria Levi asked me to support her son David on our slate and he too was elected.

Subsequently, we topped the polls and elected all three candidates every year. We were able to canvass at each branch on an organized basis and few others could really catch up. Everyone at Vancity knew that the progressive slate was the Action Slate. We were all NDP supporters and made a dent in the old armour of the incumbents by attacking their previous support of funds granted to the Fraser Institute. It is interesting to note that the Fraser Institute had earlier been created by a vice president of MacMillan Bloedel (the giant forest company) in response to the institute I had created for the Barrett government on economic policy, headed by Mason Gaffney.

Fortunately, the Vancity membership did not like their money going to right-wing causes, so in no time we were elected to the entire board every year for twenty years or more. At the very beginning, the work was not easy. The previous board and management were not on top of their lending policies, frequently lending to related partners while being unaware of their connectedness. At the beginning of the 1980s Vancity had lent excessive amounts to borrowers in the suburbs—raw landowners with no income from their vacant land ... to the point where Vancity's own soundness was threatened.

I became aware of these loans once there had been a falling out between some of the connected partners. I obtained all the details of these connected loans that threatened the very credit union itself. The board was totally unaware of the loans, who the lenders were or how weak the assets—the land—underneath the loans were. Management belatedly understood how vulnerable the credit union was once I exposed the situation to them and asked that the largest law firm attend monthly board meetings where I continued to unravel the shoddy work that management had undertaken. I was unaware that the big-time lawyer was there just for me.

In those days the board met at the Vancouver Lawn Tennis and Badminton Club and enjoyed a big dinner. I believe my reporting was a surprise to management because they themselves were unaware of the various links of the partnerships and liabilities underlying the loans. All of this caused the CEO to reconsider his job with us and he set a date to soon retire. On the last meeting of his employment, the CEO and board were advised by me of an even worse loan on the Fairview Slopes in Vancouver. In that shocking case, I uncovered a loan where the property was itself worth less than the loan by 25 percent! The CEO was leaving to take a job in Victoria that had been offered by the Socreds to head up the BC Systems Corporation, responsible for all information technology for the Province. His parting comment was that we couldn't even have a pleasant going-away meeting with him on his last day. I'm sorry, I thought, but when a banker lends out more than a property is worth, he must go before bankruptcy follows.

The irony was that those of us from a left-progressive point of view are often seen as inadequate in business but here we were having to show we knew better, cleaning up the mess left by a class of managers who were incompetent. The detailed history of all this was spelled out in *Working Dollars: The VanCity Story* by Herschel Hardin, his history of Vancity in the early days of the Action Slate. It should be required reading for all new board members. During that early period, we had to first get out of the hole that management had got us into prior to the 1981 crash in the property market, and get ourselves on a sounder banking footing. And we did. The Action Slate met every Sunday before our formal board meeting the following week, generally in Tim Louis's house in Kitsilano. I was chair for three years and Coro Strandberg was the chair for three years after that, followed by Elain Duvall. For that decade we held very tight reins on where we took our credit union. I was an executive chair, just as I had been at ICBC.

We also let our creative juices flow and sought out the best and the brightest elsewhere—where were the best community banks on the continent anyway? But before we took that big step to seek out the best models in the US to emulate, we created the Vancity Community Foundation. We wanted to establish more social planning know-how, so we donated a chunk of our profits annually to do so. Today, that capital endowment is about fifty million dollars. The initial leadership of the foundation was with David Driscoll, a former academic at Douglas College and mayor of Port Moody. In those early stages we were able to pioneer new projects with great leaders such as Al Etmanski of the Planned Lifetime Advocate Network (PLAN) who pioneered working with people with disabilities.

The PLAN folks knew that *all* of us bring a gift or gifts into the world—all of us. They fostered new friendship networks as a much more socially beneficial answer than state solutions or heavy-handed welfare. This was a new lesson for us all, prior to later learning about co-operative models in northern Italy's Emilia-Romagna region and the University of Bologna, where they had uncovered the world of reciprocity as a mutually beneficial working approach.

We also kept hearing about a community bank in Chicago that was carrying out the best community banking in the US—ShoreBank. With the board's blessing, I headed off to the Windy City to explore this reciprocity-based approach. I lined up a dinner meeting with two of the founders of ShoreBank: Mary Houghton and Ron Grzywinski. The former owners of the South Shore Bank had wanted to abandon the South Side of Chicago to move the operation downtown, away from the South Side's Black majority community. But the activist buyers wanted to keep the bank where it was and cater to the citizens on that side of the city—seeing huge opportunities to fund new Black business people who were beginning to successfully renovate the declining housing. They succeeded in acquiring the bank, keeping it in the neighbourhood and helping transform a whole community.

On that dinner date, I was able to explain to Mary Houghton what the Action Slate was all about and what we wanted to achieve. Houghton in turn was able to make it clear what she and her partners were all about: namely the rage that consumed her about the Black half of the city who were not being served by their banking system, while being surrounded by unnecessary poverty. We continued a close association with ShoreBank until they were politically assassinated once Republicans took over the treasury department.

The Action Slate in their directors' roles freed me to look at community banking in the US. As a result I spent time with the National Cooperative Bank in Washington, DC, and with the ShoreBank crew, which helped us in countless ways. We also spent time with BankBoston, aided by one of our early Action Slate directors, Steve Waddell, who was then settled there. We also met with former reps from the Santa Cruz Community Credit Union in Santa Cruz, California, including Margaret Cheap and other colleagues who were later with ShoreBank.

The ShoreBank folks were the first to alert us to the world of Bologna and Emilia-Romagna, a region of four million in the Po Valley of northern Italy. They were mainly familiar with the chamber of commerce there, which alone is very significant, but pales against the multiplicity of small family enterprises and some eight thousand co-operatives that make it one of the world's unique economies. Our first session in Bologna was with the team that created the regional development corporation plan. It was a hybrid delegation comprising a part of Vancity's board and a part of their management team, established to follow up our thoughts about a major alternative on what management had been drafting with outside consultants regarding a potential future as a federal community bank. Vancity's board had agreed to hold off on management's plan and consider my group's plan as well.

On a study tour in Emilia-Romagna, Italy, where Bob cultivated a multi-year exchange program in co-operative economics as a member of the Vancity board of directors, 2002. Bob
Williams Collection

I concluded that the consultants' plan to move us out from provincial legislation to a new federal model was unsound and risky, with
no exit strategy. The board was unsure, partly because the CEO was
so enamoured with the federal option and our CEO Bob Quart was a
Quebecer who saw things from a national viewpoint.—whereas I am a
regionalist who saw Vancity's strength as a regional player, and a proven
one. Working with John Restakis of the BC Co-operative Association,
the Action Slate was persuaded to take a serious look at Bologna and the
co-ops of Emilia-Romagna. At the beginning of the 1980s, the people of
northern Italy began an unprecedented kind of reform to address flaws
in their social delivery systems. The most advanced steps in that reform
began in the Bologna-centred region of Emilia-Romagna. The Italians
had significant doubts about huge state entities in both the social and

commercial spheres, yet were not convinced that simplistic privatization was the answer.

So, they turned to their co-operative roots to reconsider their system for managing those spheres. Built around highly skilled people and a highly diversified economy with a focus on small enterprise and co-operative enterprise, the region became one of Europe's most successful economies. Over 40 percent of its industrial products are exported and unemployment is amongst the lowest in Europe. We learned that the key to the Emilia-Romagna economy is countless small firms operating in co-operative networks. Family enterprises flourish independently but draw upon the support that co-operative networks can provide. These are networks offering private support in terms of access to capital and credit; networks that lead to certification of international exports; and networks that provide computer capacity, design assistance capacity and essential intelligence to the small enterprises.

Meanwhile, we at Vancity had seen ourselves as an interesting co-operative alternative. A group of us who worked on some of our own business and economic plans at Vancity were convinced that this co-operative institution needed to reinvent itself. We concluded that we hadn't been doing enough in terms of job creation in the Greater Vancouver region and needed to do more venturesome lending to small- and medium-sized enterprises, plus the higher-level skills of those who understood business should have been provided for the non-profit sector as well. The application of business skills in non-governmental organizations and the non-profit sector was an important new route. Indeed, after establishing the Vancity Community Foundation a decade earlier under David Driscoll, we learned that we could use grant money to build capacity and management capability in the social and non-profit sectors to the point where we could then work with such clients in a direct commercial-lending way. Vancity Capital Corporation was established to carry out venture lending for both small- and medium-sized enterprises and the non-profit sector. This was pioneering work in Canada but is old hat in Italy.

My support for decentralized approaches, which developed during my tenure as minister in the 1970s, has intensified in recent years. Through my work with Vancity and the educational program in co-operative economics at the University of Bologna, I have seen the benefits of decentralization first-hand. The Italian region of Emilia-Romagna went through a huge transformation fifty or so years ago, when the centre-left and the centre-right in Rome decided they needed to decentralize the country. These great regions of Italy, like Tuscany, Emilia-Romagna and the other subnational regions, became empowered.

Today, there's one business for every ten citizens in Emilia-Romagna. It's the most entrepreneurial place in the world! The secret of their success has been to create economic co-operative infrastructure for those countless small firms appropriate to the regions. There is a left-wing chamber of commerce, in a city of 400,000, with 700 people on staff. Those 700 people are working at creating entrepreneurial linkages between the small-business players to the point where they can produce products for export that are of very high value. It's a loose collection of free, independent players who are entrepreneurs—but they are also collectivist in the sense that they know their efforts need to be supplemented both in research and management and organizational infrastructure.

Somehow they've been able to do all that and also maintain pluralism. They ended up creating about fifteen significant research establishments for all their important sectors, from ceramics to you name it. These free-standing research agencies for each part of their regional economy became immensely proficient, so they were able to look to the future and see what kind of research work was necessary to enhance each sector. This wide range of infrastructure and co-operative activity and research lifted them all to the point where, after being decimated from the Second World War, Emilia-Romagna has become one of the wealthiest regions of Europe. It was this whole diversity that has attracted me, and which I see as part of the way to rebuild British Columbia.

I have very fond memories of the international educational program in co-operative economics that we established at Vancity in conjunction with the University of Bologna. I've said that my time at this university, probably a dozen plus trips over fifteen years, has been the most stimulating since my time at UBC planning school. "It's been like a PhD without the pain," I've told many. This experience has been a marvellous gift. John Restakis and I devised a Bologna summer program for credit union folk, NGOs and others to explore the wonder of Emilia-Romagna and its lessons pertinent to BC. I was then made senior research fellow at Vancity as a kind of goodwill gesture. In that role, I was granted a $250,000 budget to accommodate the Bologna program.

Inspired by Emilia-Romagna, we turned out the design of an economic development agency for the Lower Mainland that would see the arts as a potential driver of the regional economy. It had the blessing of Mayor Larry Campbell and involvement of the port authority and Vancouver International Airport, but there was a lack of uptake from the federal government and the Greater Vancouver Regional District (GVRD). We tend to forget that BC and the Lower Mainland is a region of small and medium enterprises, yet it is a region that doesn't have the benefit of co-operative support for such enterprises. Our strength and growth could be enhanced enormously if we did.

The essential goal of the Vancity Community Foundation is to help people help themselves. A good example of this is United We Can, a society that works with people who sort through garbage bins in the downtown alleys to pick out recyclable items that can be sold, mainly bottles and cans. The foundation loaned them operating capital to establish a recycling depot. United We Can is a great success, as are many individuals and societies that have been aided by the foundation. I am not aware of any financial institutions in the country that have created the equivalent of the Vancity Community Foundation.

During my time as chair of Vancity, we determined that once organizational performance goals were met, significant bonuses should be paid to all staff, which has continued to be the case since. We also established a subsidiary company, Vancity Enterprises, as our real estate and development arm. It had the goal of being profitable (which it was) while serving other social purposes. One of our first projects was in the 2500-block of East Hastings, the location of Vancity's third-oldest branch. We rebuilt the old branch with three floors of housing above the banking floor. The first two floors were occupied by single moms and the top floor was occupied by senior women. This project created significant social benefits while being profitable and providing us with a brand-new branch in a shopping strip that had previously been deteriorating. It won Vancity numerous awards across the US and Canada.

Although it was perilously close to receivership when I was first elected to the board, Vancity is now in excellent financial shape, and has a reputation for community service unequalled in this country. At Vancity we may have built the country's most unique financial institution, doing so over the past thirty years—working in the marketplace and increasing assets from $1.5 billion to $20 billion plus during my time there. The modern Vancity now includes:

- the Ethical Growth Fund;
- the Vancity Community Foundation;
- Vancity Enterprises;
- Vancity Regional Development Corporation;
- Vancity Capital Corporation;
- the Bologna summer program;
- the Vancity Million-Dollar Award;
- one third of profits going to members and community organizations; and
- long-standing relationship with ShoreBank in Chicago.

Virtually every major initiative for over twenty years at Vancity could be traced to the work of the Action Slate, as well as an intellectual, conceptual underpinning that arose from working with Stefano Zamagni, Vera Negri Zamagni and fellow co-operators at the University of Bologna. Like zealous bureaucrats, our fingerprints were everywhere. And we kept close control over who we put on those outside affiliated boards, including the Vancity Community Foundation. It was a slow, arduous task, but well worth it.

The credit union has a twelve-year limit for board members, which meant a curtailment of my role as director, even though I continued attending Action Slate meetings, as did Coro Strandberg. My role evolved: I became chair of Vancity Enterprises, and then I became chair of the Regional Development Corporation (RDC) task force to carry out the job of designing a business plan for the RDC (which became the Vancity Capital Corporation), and hiring a team of staff to do so.

These memories lead me to the issue of Vancity providing some funding for SFU Woodward's. It was a policy issue wrestled with by our chief executive officer, Tamara Vrooman. Vrooman privately asked me to look into the issue and come back with a recommendation. I spent time with very good staffers there, like Michael Boucher, and with Ethel Whitty, the director at Carnegie Centre, the glorious community centre in the original Carnegie Library at Main and Hastings. SFU staff had shown me rooms and facilities that could have the Vancity sponsorship name attached for anywhere from $50,000 to $10 million. I concluded our money was better for the human side—programs and outreach— and proposed $500,000. I primarily argued for outreach in Woodward's Downtown Eastside neighbourhood to overcome the rich new kid on the block stigma, and perhaps even more importantly, outreach to Carnegie, which had provided services to the regulars in the area forever. I was looking for an organic kind of marriage between the two centres. Vrooman liked what I recommended, and the board agreed.

Part of this funding was for an outreach staffer to build organic links to the neighbourhood. The actual choice of that staffer was up to SFU, fortunately, who selected Am Johal, a lad from the Cariboo who had worked for local MLA Jenny Kwan both as a minister and in the riding. They could not have made a better choice. Johal had previously embarked on our Bologna program, and also had a PhD from Switzerland in community engagement and measurement.

Jim Green loved Vancouver's inner city—he and his fellow activists redefined the neighbourhood and they gave it its current name, the Downtown Eastside. They provided new leadership and were regularly up at City Hall urging council to do anything that needed doing.

Nobody fought for housing in that neighbourhood more effectively than Green. Nobody discovered more real heroes in that neighbourhood than Green, and nobody uncovered more leaders in that small community than Green. For Green there were always new things to do. The Centre for Social Innovation in Toronto, under the management of Tonya Surman, became a new target for Green and his community. He thought it could be a goal for us in our work at Vancity.

I made a trip to Toronto to size up what these creative people were undertaking. Surman had been uncovered by the earlier work of the bold architect Margie Zeidler, who with her father had been able to rezone the old American Can factory, a large former plant with wide hallways and ceilings, two storeys in height with appealing tall windows and room for childcare and social space at the entry, bicycle sheds in the back, and space for countless activists and non-governmental organizations scattered across the breadth of their generous space, which also shared a greenhouse on the roof.

Margie Zeidler identified Surman as a key activist in the building with a natural capacity for creating clever business plans for many of the organizations. The partnership was so natural that Margie Zeidler bought another building a block along Spadina Avenue and Surman developed the business plan—for the city's new Centre for Social Innovation. A key principle of the Centre for Social Innovation was that new start-up organizations could locate there very cheaply and get help from the centre's staff organizers when they were starting up. A small office or office alcove might be available for less than $500 a month— it gave you an office and address downtown, the chance to participate with others who held similar values, meeting spaces and conference spaces that could be booked and service secretarial assistance as you needed it.

I visited them in their early stage and was greatly impressed. Surman and her team were on the second floor creating various business plans and action plans for the many NGOs and new community organizations that were tenants in the building. They had developed know-how and scale and were ready to do more. It was very appealing to undertake such a project in Vancouver's Downtown Eastside. But I unfortunately concluded that we had neither the scale, experience or people at Vancity to move so far, so fast, nor did we have a likely partner institution who might work with us. I had to advise Jim Green that we were not ready to follow through.

Green got elected to Vancouver city council and was able to get his long-awaited Woodward's project off the ground—a major mixed-market and social housing project based on the old block-and-a-half Woodward's department store site. A decade later Green would fall seriously ill and pass away quite suddenly. Those who had long partnered with Green on his many projects in the neighbourhood considered what we might do to remember him. Many of us saw the old police station at 312 Main Street as a future centre for social innovation in Vancouver. A small group that I led became the Jim Green Foundation, and set itself up to work with Vancity on that project.

With the subsequent assistance from Andy Broderick, a vice president of Vancity, we began negotiations with the City of Vancouver to negotiate a long-term lease of the former police station and prepare a plan for our own centre of social innovation. Prior to undertaking renovations, we worked with Indigenous knowledge keepers to undertake a cleansing of the building, given its history as a jailhouse where countless Indigenous people had been abused for decades. Indeed, the jails had carved walls indented with sad messages from the former occupants. The blessing ceremony was a moving sharing circle of our leadership and Indigenous leadership with drums, smoke and cedar, alternated with food and song. The windows of the building had been opened for a week to cleanse the spirits, a necessary step.

Other steps were not so carefully followed through and in the end, Vancity Community Foundation leaders and the Jim Green Foundation were moved aside for Vancity staffers to take over their work, recognizing the new financial constraints they faced. The COVID-19 pandemic created serious problems, given the financial plan was reliant on hundreds of cheap seats for the start-up NGOs. Many of the original tenants are still there: the Union of BC Indian Chiefs is up on the top floor, as are the archives of the United Church of Canada. Simon Fraser University has remained supportive of our original goals of social innovation, with Am Johal keeping a dual role both at the SFU Woodward's campus and coordinating 312 Main along with the other SFU players.

13. FIFTY YEARS LATER ... THEN AND NOW

Back in the 1970s I had concluded that the only real limit was our own imagination. It's true that, given the grandeur and opportunity that British Columbia represents, it is our own imagination that should set the limits. Some 94 percent of the province is Crown land. Humanizing our grand regions may be *the* greatest challenge in this land of abundance. Open up these tenures to real people, local people, new families for new homesteading—that could be the new great challenge in this wonderous place.

A simple scene comes to mind—on the edge of Courtenay, next to the highway, there's a thousand-acre site. It's called a woodlot. The woodlot is a licence from the Crown; two colleagues operate it. And it is the size of Stanley Park, managed for forest purposes on a sustained-yield basis. It is bigger than the fee-simple Wildwood site near Cedar, BC, where intimate care was given by one man, Merv Wilkinson, over his lifetime. These lands near Courtenay are open to local folk to enjoy the small streams and wilderness. An elderly woman is welcomed to gather salal branches for sale to local flower shops. There is money in their operating budget to fund trails and small bridges. It is quietly well managed as a forest, while welcoming local residents and generating local jobs in technology and physical labour. It is a neighbour with the spirit of generosity. There is, here, a generous love of the land and the people.

It is not centralized, corporatized or financialized as our major forest tenures are. Instead, it is simply humanized. *Go local, go small* should be our new motto. The great American essayist Wendell Berry argued that it was the paucity of imagination along with the narrow aims of the corporate world that limits us in this day and age. We don't have the human capital in the resource sector today as a result of a terribly constrained monopoly game. So, we have to rebuild a small-scale free-enterprise economy in the forest sector for it to evolve into something that's meaningful in BC's many forest-dependent communities. For this to happen, we need to decentralize the tenure and how it's managed, and start providing availability of the resource on a small scale to locally based entrepreneurs so that it starts to increase value added and incrementally builds expertise and know-how around it. And then, in an ideal world, with a good government, we'd need co-operative business infrastructure that lifts it all up beyond that level.

And so, why not more small-scale husbanding of our land? As former NDP MLA and cabinet minister Corky Evans said in one of his speeches, giant corporations dominate most of our present forest tenures and refer to these empires simply as fibre sources for their corporate machines. That's a cruel dumbing down of our glorious forest-resource heritage in this province. Of even more concern is the apparent impossibility for corporations to show love and respect for this land; it is not what they do.

The current state of the BC's forest sector demonstrates both the limitations of the existing model and the huge potential for us to do so much more. In recent years, I've devoted time and energy to forestry policy work with a circle of colleagues that included Denis O'Gorman, Ray Travers, Fred Parker, Clay Anderson and Rob Douglas, rethinking the province's biggest mess, including the historic giveaway and high grading of BC's forest resources; corporate inadequacy; the comparison with Swedish forest management over the past forty years; and the eco-forestry practices of Merv Wilkinson at Wildwood.

My current sense is that our forests don't really have a constituency anymore. We're so urban and we've licensed away ownership and control to a middling or incompetent corporate elite and absentee owners. The big tragedy of all this is that we've lost a whole rural culture and associated entrepreneurial base to manage—over 95 percent of our land base. When you think about it that way, we should all be up in arms! To illustrate, the forest sector's share of the BC economy declined from

31 percent in 1997 to 12.4 percent in 2010. Forest-sector employment declined from 115,000 in 1991 to near 40,000 in 2011. A study carried out by the great Finnish forestry consultant Jaakko Pöyry showed BC to be at the very bottom of the list amongst our peers in management capacity, workforce skill level, policy, technology and other critical factors. My associates and I feel that substantial change is essential.

I organized a group to tour the province several years back and was especially keen about stopping in Revelstoke, because I was partly responsible for getting the community tree farm licence there when I was deputy minister of Crowns. I had to push the deputy forests minister of the day into reserving the tenure around Revelstoke for the community of Revelstoke—otherwise it would have all been dissipated. It's a wonderful success story. Revelstoke's mayor at the time, Geoff Battersby, was keen about establishing this community tenure. When we visited almost thirty years later, it was really impressive. They have a log yard, allowing them to deal with their surplus timber, and a very diverse mill, Downie Street Sawmill, that is able to handle all the diverse species from that "Interior wet belt" supply area. The managers there were so smart about such difficult terrain and their unique range of species, and were getting enormous prices and values out of their cedar.

We also visited the UBC Malcolm Knapp Research Forest in the Fraser Valley; the College of New Caledonia Research Forest in Prince George; mills in Prince George, Revelstoke and Midway; operators in the Cariboo; the mayor of Quesnel; the Creston Community Forest; community forests in several other towns; and other mills on Vancouver Island. In 2018, I was subsequently invited by the Canadian Centre for Policy Alternatives to write a report, *Restoring Forestry in BC: The story of the industry's decline and the case for regional management*, where I indicated some of the new steps in forest policy that we considered helpful, including:

- a forester general as a servant of the legislature who would report annually for each of the six macro-regions of the province to legislative committees of the House comprised of local MLAS;

- a legislated Forest Charter to articulate overall goals and purposes relative to achieving improved forest resources;
- an up-to-date, renewed and regularly managed inventory refined as the foundational scientific database under the oversight of the forester general;
- a regional level of resource development governance modelled after the Columbia Basin Trust within the great macro-region of the Kootenays;
- macro-region committees of the House that could be linkages and feedback loops between the macro-regions for increased coordination; and
- greater local control and management, including many more local community forests modelled on the experience and success of the Mission Municipal Forest, the Revelstoke Community Forest and other tenures populating our hinterland in a diverse way.

In 1972 we were a federation of reformers who were elected. Each of us carried the hopes and dreams of those who had gone before. We each brought our own people with us. We found our own people to determine our own priorities and pursue them. Some departments of government had their plans on the shelf, plus a few relied on former ministers, while others had no capacity to analyze themselves. After twenty long years of Socred control, a housecleaning was required. I believe that we may have been the most thoughtful, questioning, and at the same time, the boldest government in the history of our young province. We looked at everything in depth, and with Dave Barrett as premier, we all had fun doing it. And the dirty dozen of us reflected the wonderful diversity of the province.

After our first year in government in 1972 we were ready to empower others: real people in the regions who were ready to grow and provide a new kind of governance for us all. We had to use our power in Victoria to limit direct use of power and instead shift it to real communities in the cities and the regions. Had we been given a second term back then, there is little doubt that the new government's direction might well have been determined by Norman Levi and me, who saw more local control as the goal we should seek. The bureaucratic hierarchy rarely delivered; however, we had had the good fortune of inheriting a tiny civil service and thus were unencumbered. We failed to realize what a threat our approach would be to future incumbent bureaucracies, who are generally unprepared for creative change.

With his executive assistants Ray Wargo and Joe Denofreo, Levi had already concluded that within our major cities there was a need for community resource boards and had begun setting them up with flexibility to respond to neighbourhood needs and goals. The needs in Hastings East clearly differed from those in Point Grey. I was not as far advanced in decentralization as Levi, but had begun to respond to folks in the West Kootenays, specifically in the Slocan Valley. From our different stations in human resources and natural resources, each of us had independently realized that *the* big job we had at the provincial level was to empower local communities—that it was the community level that best represented the people.

We concluded that the traditional public service was near useless in delivering what we needed for these actions. We had to innovate. For example, in Burns Lake, we empowered local First Nations and Métis by establishing the Burns Lake Native Development Corporation to operate a new sawmill. We had to search out local people to train members of the local First Nation and we equipped a small college in Prince George to certify them. I had been impressed by Mission in the Fraser Valley, where the local government managed their own municipal tree farm with smarts and initiative, becoming the first people on this coast of North America to learn how to propagate yellow cedar. Yellow cedar was hardy and could grow in the cold, windy crags north of Mission.

The Slocan was an area I'd worked in as a Forest Service summer employee. The population was a wonderful mix of former Americans (Vietnam objectors) and Doukhobors, descendants of religious dissidents who had been repressed in Eastern Europe. It was a subregion generally dismissed as not having enough human capital to pull itself up by its own bootstraps. However, young people in the valley had obtained an early federal government Opportunities for Youth (OFY) grant, and carried out an analysis and history of economic development and resource management in their valley. It was a superb report; no local plans have been equalled before or since.

The report recommended local control of forest management in the valley and value-added production based on the harvest. I was sold on it and decided we should begin decentralization efforts there. Toward the end of our tenure as government, we had begun the process of experimenting with local control and management, setting up a local natural resource management group for the full Slocan Valley extending from Nakusp down through to Castlegar.

The young former American who headed that OFY study was Corky Evans, who later became NDP MLA for Nelson–Creston and a cabinet minister in the 1990s. In a recent essay called "Tragedy of the Commons," he reflects upon the opportunity we provided him and his colleagues in local control of management:

> I want to argue that this is the moment in our history where we might want our government to change direction and work with communities, rather than capital, to manage the resources in their territories. The corporation (who brought the capital) gradually eliminated the public from access to the timber—it became a deal between Victoria, with all the power, and the companies that worked the land, with all the money. Eventually the rules around government's right to control the sale of assets to limit spectators were removed and now we are living in a time of utter corporate control over forest land and forest policy... Corporate consolidation [of the forest sector] has wiped out the employment base all over BC putting the interests of capital over the interest of the people who live where the resources are harvested ... Bob changed his mind forty-five years ago [to endorse greater

local control] and the tragedy of the Commons is when
resources are taken away from local people and managed
at a distance!

This view that has been reinforced especially by all that has been
accomplished in Revelstoke by Mayor Geoff Battersby and his exercise
of local control. Evans carries on in this essay to celebrate the Columbia
Basin Trust, which could become a model for the province. BC is a province of regions that are currently governed from afar in truly Victorian
buildings south of the forty-ninth parallel. There is Vancouver Island,
the Lower Mainland, the Southern Interior, the Kootenays, the Cariboo, the Thompson Okanagan, the Chilcotin, North Coast–Nechako
and the Peace. Is it not time that each of these regions participated in its
own governance?

Vancouver Island is clearly near the top of the list as a great region
itself. History alone defines it, as do its people. And some of the big
issues, such as First Nations reconciliation and land settlements,
appear to be more graspable and manageable, and thus appropriate to
be addressed at the local level. The largest First Nation of Vancouver
Island—the Cowichan people—were squeezed into some of the tini-
est reserves in the province by the early enormous land grants to the
Esquimalt and Nanaimo Railway, in exchange for establishing a small
and ultimately failing railway on the Island.

Now encompassing much of southeast Vancouver Island, those earlier land grants usurp the traditional Indigenous lands of the Cowichan Valley, leaving this great First Nation surviving on postage-stamp
reserves around the City of Duncan. Land reform and reallocation
is long overdue. These lands could be allocated and become a combination of woodlots for First Nations, spiritual and historic lands;
operating forests; municipal tree farms; diverse woodlots and small
holdings. The potential abundance for the people of South Vancouver
Island through such diversification and local management would be
enormous. Diversity and a greater love and respect for the land would
prevail to benefit us all. Creating an independent forest charter for

Vancouver Island within a Vancouver Island trust for forest governance jointly with the Island's regional districts and First Nations would be an exciting beginning toward righting the wrong of the original Esquimalt and Nanaimo Railway land grant, creating new custodians for the management and protection of those lands.

Think of other regions—the Shuswap Country, the Fraser Canyon, the South Cariboo, the Chilcotin. We can enrich ourselves spiritually and financially by similarly reopening these regions to diversity and humanizing these glorious spaces. These giant lands could have a new land-use management and settlement pattern at a local scale, with opportunities available to new generations who might well create more thoughtful, enduring, sustainable and loving environments. The boldest decision of the Barrett government in the 1970s was to wipe the rules clean on agricultural lands, put them in limit under that statute and advance new rules through cabinet order, enabling the ongoing protection of those lands under the new Agricultural Land Commission.

And then there are our mountains...We somehow ignore proper planning for their use and management. It may be because we've leased them out so deeply to giant forest companies who unfortunately describe them as fibre for low-value processing. These big companies seem to have purposely dumbed down the definitions of this magnificent landscape so that we fail to see what a misallocation it has been, and fail to understand how cheaply we have let our mountains go into forest company lands with inadequate attention to watershed, wildlife habitat, conservation, outdoor recreation, and potential visual and scenic values.

A little-known story is Al Raine's dream of developing another major ski resort, still in the Coastal Mountains but on the edge of Lillooet where there was dry Interior snow. He had searched for this somewhat hidden valley for some time, while being sure it was there. On one fly-over, the clouds parted and he spotted it—Cayoosh Creek. He prepared a proposal and got initial support of the Cayoose Creek Band and the Lil'wat First Nation, then commenced a dialogue with the provincial civil service. It was a convoluted process that took almost a decade of changing demands from inadequate government staff. The bureaucrats finally granted their approval, but by then the ship had sailed ... far from the high-capacity experience he had when getting Whistler established.

Subsequently, Raine was invited by Japanese investors to rethink the possibilities of upgrading and expanding Mount Tod near Kamloops. Raine was able to guide them on the resort now called Sun Peaks, developing it into its amazing present status as Canada's second-largest ski area, some 4,270 acres of skiable area over three peaks. In the past decade, he attracted new funds to build a convention centre in the heart of the village, generating new year-round activity.

While Raine was deprived of his own second act at Cayoosh Creek, he delivered the bolder second act of Sun Peaks. Shouldn't governments ask one of BC's greatest citizens, Al Raine, "What more do you see out there in the ski business?" I asked Raine that question just a few years ago and I am still excited by his responses, including one of which I was totally unaware. An area near the Coquihalla Summit topped his substantial list. Like Blackcomb, logging was planned near a site with a significant potential near the extraordinary new route to the Interior, the Coquihalla. But it was not pursued.

Is there another model around somewhere in the world that British Columbia might emulate? Yes, there is. It is the Dolomites in Northern Italy. This region is also referred to as the South Tyrol and has been governed by Italy since the settlement of border issues after the First World War. It is a region living in harmony with the skills of their two peoples: Austrians and Italians. I inquired of Carlo Borzaga, a local academic, how they managed this magnificent mountain region for generations post-1918. His response was that their national government in Rome saw their border region as needing careful attention and specific infrastructure policies.

In touring the Dolomites, I was greatly impressed by the fact that most of the mountain villages had unique adjacent peaks that were almost all accessed by a major lift or aerial tramway from the centre of the village to those peaks. The operation of the facility was cooperatively accommodated by the local village and businesses.

When in the Dolomites, one finds it quite apparent that the economy of this very large region is created by the linkage between the vertical movement of visitors to their glorious mountaintops and alpine meadows, and to the private enterprise services and amenities—the hotels and restaurants—of the hospitality folks in the villages below. Who paid for this grand infrastructure? The national government in Rome paid for 60 percent of the capital cost and the local community paid the balance.

Shouldn't the mountain regions of BC be seen in the same light? We have federal spending on our horizontal highway system, but no federal spending on our vertical system. Is there not a potential case for both? There is a huge business case for the vertical transportation up the mountains to transform our hinterland. The mix of land, labour, private capital and community capital in the spectacular Interior of our province needs to be adjusted and once we understand that, along with a rethinking of forest tenures, we will be on our way to creating a new and more diversified economy for ourselves.

When I was first elected as an MLA I took a tour way up Island with Walter Kozij, the IWA organizer for that region. I was amazed that there was a gate across the provincial highway at Campbell River, placed there by the then dominant forest company in that part of the Island, Canfor (Canadian Forest Products). Like everybody else, we had to pay a toll to use their road to get up to Port Hardy. The only settlement at that time in that long distance was a temporary company townsite—Woss Camp.

Woss Camp might well have been a permanent town, yet it was not. As a planner interested in settlement, I enquired of my economic advisor Mason Gaffney why the company would do this. Gaffney's response was that there was a similar pattern in the eastern US—in northern Maine near the Canadian border. He figured the reason was the companies did not want to have to pay taxes. These corporations knew that if they had substantial settlements in their regions, the citizens who were there would want various urban services, utilities, health, education and social services—and so, they avoided having any town within their tenures. I realized he was right.

When I got back from that tour, I argued in the legislature that right there on Vancouver Island, we were a banana republic. Every loaf of bread and litre of milk was taxed at the gate at Campbell River: a levy on the folks of Port Hardy and Port McNeill by Canfor. Even worse, the cost of building that highway was deducted from the royalty or tax that Canfor paid for their logs... So, in truth, the road had been paid for by the Forest Service of British Columbia. Therefore, we the citizens had paid for that road! After my speech in the legislature, the gate on the highway was removed within the month.

The lack of settlement in so much of BC is rooted in the excessive power we have given the forest corporations, letting them break social contracts, or allowing them to simply do nothing. Underneath it all is the rent-seeking game. Few economists are aware of how significant this economic rent is. Over a century ago, it was celebrated as *the* most important issue by Henry George, who defined it for the Western world in his great book *Progress and Poverty*. Those days the debate was between the Marxists, the capitalists, the social democrats and the followers of Henry George. I found myself hovering between the social democrats and the Georgists and with a real sympathy for co-operators.

Throughout this book there have been many references to economic rent. The main elements of the economy are land, labour and capital. The study of economic rent is relatively new. An excellent review of early thinking in the evolution of the economics discipline is covered by the Italian economist Mariana Mazzucato in her book *The Value of Everything*, where she describes a brief history of value. The answer lies in the soil (or land) and then classical economics: value in labour. She notes that the study of rent has disappeared in modern times while it was of a primary interest at the time of Adam Smith, when early intellects reflected on these elements of production and issues such as unearned increment in land where landowners made money "even when they slept."

Henry George, the pioneering American economist, became the champion of the rent issue, arguing that the grand settlement of the West was a means of acquiring equity in land when none was available in the east of the country. The rent issue became the great debate of those days. George argued that rent—economic rent—was probably the fairest revenue for government. Taxes on labour and capital had a negative effect on the use of capital and labour, whereas a tax on rent was the incentive to get land and resources employed and, in effect, put into production. In George's time there were competing arguments for socialism, communism, co-operatives and the land tax or collecting rent for the common good.

Modern economists have failed to be concerned with tracking the data in terms of rent year by year. In BC, where the Province owns 94 percent of the land, we do not even include those lands in our provincial budget as part of our balance sheet. What company in our society would be so sloppy in accounting for their own assets? None. I asked a former deputy minister of finance for BC why that was so. She replied that she had asked the same question of an earlier deputy in that ministry. He replied that they sort of kept it in reserve when dealing with bond agents in New York. If their numbers in the budget were being questioned, they would reply, "Oh, but we have all our provincial lands." No more questions were asked.

The failure to track these values annually means we do not collect information that is critical. We lease these lands out to forest companies. It is probably the case that these lease rates are so low that they are in fact lowering the book value of these lands. In this day and age, to know that we are doing that to ourselves is a shocking reality. In the case of private lands, I was able to convince our government that we had to build up an annual database for all urban and private lands in the province. Thus, we established the BC Assessment Authority, which is responsible for the market assessment of all privately held land and buildings in the province. These assessments are the basis for all municipal and regional property taxation in the province. The agency is considered by its peers as the best agency of its kind in all of North America.

Real property (land and buildings) is valued annually, on a market basis, for the tax rolls. One of our intentions when we established the agency was to have a superb database that we could analyze. We now have that. Indeed, when I wanted to carry out an analysis of our downtown areas in Vancouver and Victoria in the mid-1990s, I was able to pull out information that I do not believe has been obtained before by others in other major cities. I was able to obtain the information on the entire cash flow out of the commercial sections of the Vancouver downtown peninsula and compare it to the civic budget. I found that that cash flow exceeded the entire civic budget by 50 percent! Those facts and others provided material for a major speech I gave to the Union of Russian Mayors in Moscow in the 1990s. We now look at the huge invasion of external capital in our land market, and we can figure it out.

At the time of our study in the 1990s, we discovered that the Burrard Peninsula of the Greater Vancouver area had land values that grew twelve-fold in the previous dozen years. Most impressive, however, was the land value in Surrey, which had increased at double that rate—twenty-four-fold over the same period! What no one seems to understand is that the growth of values since then has probably quadrupled again. The largest ethnic minority group that had moved to Surrey in those years were South Asians who bought up small acreages near Whalley and along Scott Road (120 Street). These folks were the primary beneficiaries of what may have been the greatest transfer of wealth in British Columbia's history.

I am especially pleased with the agency we created in the 1970s, which Dave Barrett had agreed we should do, creating one of the best land databases in the world. And it was ready for the oncoming invasion of new capital post-1975. Mason Gaffney was the intellectual behind this work, bringing in an assessor-appraiser from Indiana who had recently established a new agency there to focus on land-value changes. Between new Georgist American know-how and incumbent skilled British property appraisers, we formed an invaluable team to carry out this important exercise. These urban land values increase in the trillions, and much of the unearned increment of new land values is now being transferred abroad to the new foreign landowners.

Elsewhere in this book I have covered other examples of rent—the most egregious example of stolen rent is on the Kootenay River tributary of the Columbia River. The power from that river's licensees was extended in perpetuity to Cominco, the owners of the large smelter in Trail, BC, for nothing. In the same region, the Province shared some of the available rent from the river in the Columbia Basin directly to the people of the region via the Columbia Basin Trust. Just think of what sharing such rent opportunities throughout the province in a similar manner would yield!

The nature of economic rent in our society is as relevant as ever—even though it now gets buried in the modern world of financialization and the acronym FIRE (finance, insurance and real estate) used by the bureaucrats. It is now the resident area for the great economic freeloaders in our society.

A Canadian politician who has shown some sympathy for Henry George is the current federal finance minister, Chrystia Freeland. She gives a glimpse of that in her 2012 book, *Plutocrats*. In the introduction of that book, Freeland notes that George was such a firm believer in free enterprise that he opposed the income tax. For him, Freeland notes, "the emergence of plutocrats, the robber barons, was the 'Great Sphinx.' 'This association of poverty with progress,' he wrote, 'is the great enigma of our times... So long as all the increased wealth which modern progress brings goes but to build up great fortunes, to increase luxury and make sharper the contrast between the House of Have and the House of Want, progress is not real and cannot be permanent.'" As Freeland remarks, "A century and a half later, that Great Sphinx has returned." As Freeland notes, so much of rent-seeking has now gone global; she argues that the great danger today is "the rise of an international rent-seeking global oligarchy." Amen!

And what about the Lower Mainland? We in Greater Vancouver have seen this pattern accelerate in our own property market. In my lifetime here, I have seen Bob Lee develop the first major China transactions; Lee spoke Cantonese and made the first big deals with Chinese capital and then went on to share his great knowledge with the UBC board of governors for the UBC property endowment fund, which is expected to grow to $4 billion in value for the university. That's capturing future rent for public benefit. But the rent value of urban property in the Lower Mainland has grown by trillions over the years since our Expo 86 brought us new attention from the world's rent seekers. Rent seekers saw our downtown as the great generator of rent. More and more Asian investors wanted to capture the long-term rent of our downtown. We subsequently looked at the smaller Victoria downtown. Here again we found the cash flow in their central business district to be 150 percent of their normal annual property tax income for the remainder of the city. We sensed we might be uncovering a general principle about the giant value of our downtowns.

Although the belly of BC houses our greatest opportunities, it is nearly matched by the near wasteland of False Creek Flats. I argued when I was on city council for the new possibilities that Mayor Art Phillips and his team led by Walter Hardwick and Geoff Massey pursued— the barrel maker at the north end of the Cambie Bridge was terminated, along with the forest industry uses with log booms and burners. The south side became an attractive new community with co-op housing and a new Granville Island.

But east of Main Street has remained almost vacant: a railway yard little changed from when it was built a century ago. It was political drive that rebuilt west of Main, and now we need a new drive and know-how to rebuild east of Main. It is extraordinary that this anomaly east of Main Street continues. The railway companies are content with the way things are, and need to be involved in the change. The North–South BNSF Railway line that links the Grandview cut to the Burrard Inlet and our main port is limited, crowded and underdeveloped. Strengthening that line, and possibly covering it, is overdue. The spaghetti pattern of railyards to the east and Main Street needs to be rethought.

The glorious central business district of Vancouver is a stone's throw away from these few hundred acres in the underdeveloped flats. The lack of political will in cleaning this mess up remains a shocker. The land values west of Main Street are enormous, while the land values east of Main are dismal. There is so much to be gained by pursuing the transition. At an earlier stage the old creeks that tumbled down to the flats got encased in giant sewers that might yet be opened and day-lighted, adding even more to the new land values that are waiting to be uncovered and enhanced again, by water. This significant area can still be transformed; it just needs the will!

Thinking back over this period of my life and the life of our province, it's a reminder of just how powerful institutions and cultures are, and generally how slow they are to change. My reference to Vancouver City Hall and other institutions may seem a little cruel. But I've worked at and watched that place for a lifetime, and it's one powerful culture. All those senior bureaucrats train each new councillor coming up, feeding them information bit by bit. Controlling information, managing information, is a major source of their power. I welcomed it with the Non-Partisan Association, who were trained bit by bit by bureaucrats ready to anoint their own new mayor. I've seen it more recently with councillors from the centre and left. Same process: training them, the councillors, about *process—their* game.

Even in Victoria, bureaucrats briefed *us* about the rules, for God's sake. They would be offended when *I* was offended. And you'd think with all the partisan executive assistants that arrive in Victoria, and the building up of the premier's office staff, a lot would change. It might for a little while at the beginning of a term, but then it's institutional business as usual. And that's not even considering leaked information and sabotage, which are the biggest weapons in the bureaucratic arsenal. Also, politicians never learn not to love having their asses kissed. We're all human after all, and it's nice to hear that *you* are the greatest minister they've ever had. After a while you believe it.

Reflecting on all this now, how from 1972–1975 we politicians were in most ways in complete control of processes and the province's destiny, I recall Dave Barrett saying, "Williams, there's never been a government like us in all of history." At the time, I was inclined to dismiss Barrett's hyperbole. But on reflection, Barrett was so right! Looking at the world today, I'm saddened by the bureaucratization of all things: how apparatchiks dominate the political scene, and most everything gets watered down, cleansed for political correctness, making sure that no fire or passion escapes from politicians' mouths. Harshness, honesty, passion and immediacy tend to disappear under formulaic, careful, uncontroversial commentary. We are all the losers in the hands of these new bureaucratic power managers in the back room. That's not to say that bureaucrats are all bad. They're not. Some are superb. But good ones are unfortunately rare birds.

Institutions always bother me. Institutions always get corrupted. Labour has been corrupted as an institution, in my view, just as churches have, and so many other things. Do unions really think of themselves as saviours of the working class? I'm not so sure. They become institutions with their own specific interests. They're simply union-dues collectors in a narrow way, and they're the mirror image of the corporations they're a part of.

Similarly, I have never been that impressed with our captains of industry. After all, look what I as an amateur had been able to achieve with Canadian Cellulose, Columbia Cellulose and the wonderful Ray Jones. A former vice president of the Powell River Company, Jones left that company after it merged with MacMillan Bloedel, where he rightly couldn't stand J.V. Clyne, then chair of the board and a former BC Supreme Court judge. Clyne of course was emblematic of the coming sickness in the industry. Jones went on to work for the E.B. Eddy Company in Quebec and then Garfield Weston in the UK, before coming to run our new forestry assets in the 1970s.

Back in my younger years, before my marriage and political career, I hadn't acknowledged the fact that I was gay. It wasn't relevant then, or didn't seem to be. In fact I had a passionate affair with one of my female secretaries, who was married at the time. We took a day off and went to my buddies' mountain cabin up on Hollyburn Mountain and made love. She separated, got a job at Vancouver City Hall, and we saw each other over the years. But sweet as she was, we were not a match. Intellectually, it was problematic. That sounds so snobbish, I know, but there was a big gap. Another female colleague who knew about the relationship would say to me, "Be realistic Bob. It won't work out. What do you have to talk about after sex anyway?"

In truth, I'd harboured a passion for a young East Side buddy who was raised by his grandparents on nearby Nanaimo Street, Bill Hammond. The old folks still kept chickens in the basement back then. My other closest friend, Ray Holmes, lived nearby in the 2500-block of Parker in a tiny four-room house. Holmes's room was in the basement, a few planks over a dirt floor. It was a very working-class neighbourhood then. All of us—Bill Hammond, Ray Holmes, Bill Boutilier and I— would hang out on the Inlet with our inexpensive boats that we moored at a squatter marina in Barnet in North Burnaby.

Young Bill Hammond was as handsome as a young man gets. We'd often go down to the Princeton Hotel nearby on an idle evening and walk back to the Wall Street house. But young Hammond was straight as an arrow, unfortunately. He married Joan, one of the women he met up Hollyburn Mountain, and as far as I know, lived happily ever since. The last time I saw Hammond was after a Britannia Secondary School reunion.

I learned over time that the job of the good politician was to use power well. When I was in Key West writing these memoirs, I reflected on the 1930s, when the great American president FDR built his favourite Works Progress Administration (WPA) project—the road link to Key West—putting unemployed people to work connecting their communities and building their country. I reflected on the need for a new WPA to meet the challenges in our twenty-first-century world—attacking Depression-like conditions by empowering, revitalizing and transforming individuals, communities and regions.

In my own case, I believe I used power well. I enlisted the professionals who were best in their fields—economists, planners, lawyers, social workers, consultants—always wanting to know the norms to try to work within them, even on radical projects, but always informed by a sense of history, roots and the public interest. Alistair Crerar was there with his great skills and experience on projects like the Burns Lake Native Development Corporation, where he insisted upon the best commercial lawyers to protect the Indigenous Peoples.

Today, government intervention is needed on a renewed, grand scale in British Columbia and across the world—in banking and finance, obviously, as well as in other sectors, expanding people-centred co-operative economics and breaking up the big banks and other corporate conglomerations of power and wealth. From my own work in government intervention—Whistler, Robson Square, Surrey City Centre—I know a modern WPA would be wonderful.

Two vignettes highlight for me the benefits of this people-centred approach. The first is from a speech I gave a few years ago at Simon Fraser University's downtown campus in the Harbour Centre. To my amazement about sixty people showed up. The subject was economic democracy. During the speech, I talked about Vancity and its role, and Italy and Bologna and the history of co-operatives there—amazing experiences all over the place. Afterwards, one of the Downtown Eastside folks came up to me and said how lucky I was to have had the range of experiences I'd talked about. And she was right.

A few months later, I was on my way to another event at Simon Fraser University's Woodward's arts centre. I stopped on Carrall Street, looking up at a neon sign for the rehabilitated Rainier Hotel. And I looked farther down the street toward the rehabilitated Pennsylvania Hotel. It too had a grand neon sign. Both places provide social housing. It was almost dusk, with the lights and the wet streets reflecting them, beautiful in the Vancouver way. I was reflecting, as a policy wonk is wont to do, on the costs of those signs versus more money for basic housing needs. And I was leaning in the direction of basic housing needs.

I didn't notice a woman not far away from me, watching me watching the sign! When I looked down and realized she was there, she said to me, "Aren't they beautiful?" She was obviously a woman of modest means who lived there in the Downtown Eastside.

I was stunned silent for a moment. Then I smiled at her, and I said, "Yes, yes they are." I thought to myself, why should she not have beauty in her life?

Our job is to use power well.

INDEX

Page numbers in bold refer to photographs.

ABOUT THE AUTHORS

Bob Williams is a former British Columbia cabinet minister who played a key role in establishing the Agricultural Land Reserve and Insurance Corporation of British Columbia during BC's first NDP government in the late 1970s. More recently, Williams was influential in building the Vancity Credit Union into the leading co-operative financial institution in Western Canada.

Benjamin Isitt is a historian and legal scholar specializing in the political and legal history of British Columbia's working class, with previous works including *From Victoria to Vladivostok* (UBC Press, 2010) and *Able to Lead* (UBC Press, 2021). He also serves as a city councillor and regional director in Victoria, BC.

Thomas Bevan is an urban planner working to develop affordable housing and living in Vancouver's West End. He grew up in downtown Kitchener, Ontario, and has studied cities and real estate values.